# MODERN
# ENGLISH  ESSAYS

### EDITED BY ERNEST RHYS

# MODERN
# ENGLISH ESSAYS

## VOLUME FOUR

E. V. LUCAS
J. MASEFIELD
W. L. COURTNEY
H. W. NEVINSON
ARTHUR WAUGH
EDWARD THOMAS
SIR OLIVER LODGE
BRANDER MATTHEWS
R. B. CUNNINGHAME GRAHAM
RICHARD LE GALLIENNE
L. PEARSALL SMITH
H. W. MASSINGHAM
G. K. CHESTERTON
JOSEPH CONRAD
HILAIRE BELLOC
FIONA MACLEOD
T. SECCOMBE
E. RHYS

1922
LONDON & TORONTO
J. M. DENT & SONS LTD.
NEW YORK: E. P. DUTTON & CO.

# EDITOR'S NOTE

EIGHTEEN essayists are grouped together in this volume, and it would be idle to say they are of one school, or intrinsically of the same character. They range from Edward Verrall Lucas, whose "Philosopher that Failed" comes from his *Character and Comedy*, to Logan Pearsall Smith, whose essay on the Rose is from *Trivia*. These are both books of one period, given to brief considerations of things; yet they are markedly diverse. One writer is a relisher of life and letters; the other, a spiritual sybarite. The latter is an American by birth; so is Professor Brander Matthews, whose function as professor and New York dramatic critic has not spoilt his hand as an essayist. His account of Maria Edgeworth is an "Everyman" essay. Another contributor is Hilaire Belloc. He has written books *On Nothing* (1907), *On Everything* (1909), and *On Anything* (1910). His essays here printed come from the first of the three. He and his congenial fellow prose-writer, G. K. Chesterton, who contributes two essays, write from the life and from the hour, much as did the eighteenth-century men. Joseph Conrad does not occur to us first as an essayist;

yet his *Mirror of the Sea*, an essayist's book, is the most intimate of all his works, and his tribute in it to "The West Wind" a rare bit of eloquence. Here his tribute is to his old masters in the sea-tale, Marryat and Fenimore Cooper, from his *Notes on Life and Letters*. Other estimates and critical appreciations include Thomas Seccombe on a congenial theme, Mrs. Gaskell's *Mary Barton*; John Masefield on the Pilgrim Fathers, and Sir Oliver Lodge on Huxley.

Of the remaining contributors, two, H. W. Massingham and Henry W. Nevinson, serve to call up another review, *The Nation and Athenæum*, which has maintained the periodical essay with some verve. *The Fortnightly Review* comes into the record again with its editor's characteristic appreciation of Miss Mary Wilkins. Cunninghame Graham's essay, "The Grey Kirk," reminds us that he was an old *Scots Observer* contributor, and carries us north. Fiona Macleod held a region apart from which come "The Hill-Tarn" and "Winter Stars." Two writers who recall English scenes remain: the late Edward Thomas, who died, alas! in a foreign field and loved equally Welsh and English countrysides; and Mr. Arthur Waugh, a cordial critic and a Wessex man, whose account of "The City of Bath" comes from his book *Reticence in Literature*.

For the kind permission to use copyright essays in this volume, full and special acknowledgments are due to:

Mr. Hilaire Belloc and Messrs. Methuen and Co. for "On an Unknown Country" and "On the Approach of an Awful Doom."

Mr. G. K. Chesterton for "A Defence of Nonsense" and a Dickens essay.

Mr. Joseph Conrad for "Tales of the Sea."

Mr. W. L. Courtney and Messrs. Chapman and Hall for "Miss Mary Wilkins."

Mr. Cunninghame Graham and Mr. Duckworth for "The Grey Kirk."

Mr. Richard Le Gallienne and Mr. John Lane for "The Dream Children of Literature."

Mr. E. V. Lucas and Messrs. Methuen for "A Philosopher that Failed" (from *Character and Comedy*).

Mr. H. W. Massingham and *The Nation and Athenæum* for "Shaw and Swift."

Mr. H. W. Nevinson and *The Nation and Athenæum* for "Of Comfort."

Mrs. William Sharp and Messrs. Heinemann for "The Hill-Tarn" and "Winter Stars," by Fiona Macleod (William Sharp).

Mr. Logan Pearsall Smith, Messrs. Constable, and Messrs. Doubleday, Page and Co. for "The Rose," from *Trivia*.

*The Nineteenth Century and After* for "The Death of Swinburne."

Mr. Arthur Waugh for "The City of Bath."

The remaining essays from "Everyman's Library" and other volumes in Messrs. Dent's list are reprinted by the courtesy of Sir Oliver Lodge, Mr. Masefield, Mr. Seccombe, and Mr. Edward Thomas.

# CONTENTS

# MODERN ENGLISH ESSAYS

## A PHILOSOPHER THAT FAILED

### By E. V. Lucas

Of Oliver Edwards, nothing, I believe, is known beyond the fact that he had been at Pembroke College with Dr. Johnson; that he was a solicitor in Barnard's Inn; that he married twice; that he lived on a little farm of sixty acres near Stevenage and came to London twice a week; and that he wore grey clothes and a wig with many curls, and went to church on Good Fridays. We know of Edwards's life only this, and of his speech we have only some dozen sentences; and yet he will live for ever, by virtue of having crossed the stage of literature on one fine morning one hundred and twenty-nine years ago. He might be likened to the bird with which the Venerable Bede compared the life of man in a famous and beautiful passage: the bird that flies out of the dark void into the lighted banqueting hall and out again into the void once more. So with Edwards: for sixty years he was not; then he met Dr. Johnson and his Boswell in Butcher Row, stayed with them for an

hour; and was not again. But the hour was
sufficient: it gave him time to make his one
deathless remark. By virtue of that remark he
lives, and will live.

Edwards's day was Good Friday, 17th April,
1778—"a delightful day," says Boswell. How
little the good Edwards can have thought, as he
climbed out of his bed in Barnard's Inn that
morning and donned his grey clothes and his curly
wig, that he was about to become immortal. He
spent, I take it, the early hours in his office, reading
conveyances or deeds and writing letters; then he
went to church, whither Dr. Johnson and Boswell
had also gone, to St. Clement's, which through
some strange stroke of luck is standing, with
the Doctor's pew intact within it, to this dark,
irreverent, rebuilding day.

On the way Boswell (who could grow the flower
quite easily now, having obtained much seed)
remarked that Fleet Street was the most cheerful
scene in the world, adding, skilfully as he thought,
" Fleet Street is, in my mind, more delightful than
Tempe!" The Doctor, however, having the same
dislike of the imitator that most teachers and all
cynics possess, had his dash of cold water ready.
" Ay, ay, but let it be compared with Mull." So
they passed on to church, where the Doctor was
pleased to see so numerous a congregation.

It was after church that they met Edwards,
whom Johnson had not seen for forty years. The
recognition came from the lawyer, a talkative,

friendly, and not easily daunted man, who thereafter quickly got to work and enlarged to Boswell on the pleasure of living in the country. Boswell, again in the true Johnsonian manner, replied, " I have no notion of this, sir. What you have to entertain you is, I think, exhausted in half an hour." But Edwards was deeper and more sincere. " What," he said, " don't you love to have hope realised? I see my grass, and my corn, and my trees growing. Now, for instance, I am curious to see if this frost has not nipped my fruit trees." Johnson, who had been in a reverie, possibly missing the familiar scent of incense—for, in spite of Boswell's innuendoes to the contrary, Edwards does not appear to have been at all impressed by the magnitude and lustre of his old friend—here remarked, " You find, sir, you have fears as well as hopes "; and I am glad he did so, for it gave Boswell the opportunity to add the reflection, " So well did he see the whole when another saw but the half of a subject." And yet it is more than likely that Edwards saw the whole too.

Being comfortably seated in the Bolt Court library on this sunny Good Friday, Edwards, who had already commented with delightful bluntness, but perfect innocence, on the Doctor's age, remarked, " Sir, I remember you would not let us say ' prodigious ' at college. For even then," he added, turning to Boswell " he was delicate in language, and we all feared him." Johnson said nothing of this at the time, but to his Boswell said afterwards, in private, " Sir, they respected me for my literature "—meaning by " they " the undergraduates—" and yet it was not great but by comparison. Sir, it is amazing how little literature there is in the world." That was one hundred and twenty-nine years ago, and it is amazing still.

The conversation with Edwards then turned to money, and it came out that the lawyer had given much away. He also admitted to a longing to be a parson and live in comfort and comparative idleness. Johnson had an opening here, and took it. " I would rather have Chancery suits upon my hands," he said, " than the cure of souls. No, sir, I do not envy a clergyman's life as an easy life, nor do I envy the clergyman who makes it an easy life." Edwards, however, did. There is no evidence that the Doctor convinced him. My impression is that he was never convinced by anyone's arguments. I picture him as the kind of man who goes through life contentedly, secure in his own opinion.

Nothing could daunt Edwards, and so innocent and happy was he that he had no notion he was not observing the strict rules of the game. The rules of the Johnson conversational game made it imperative that you should utter only questions or provocative opinions, and then wait for the answer and receive it humbly. But Edwards smilingly broke them all. He asked questions, it is true, but long before the Doctor could reply he had volunteered, with appalling hardihood, scraps of

4

autobiography.  If there is one thing an auto-
biographer like Johnson cannot stand it is the
autobiography of others.  And yet the Doctor,
with his great human imagination, knew that
Edwards was a pearl of sincerity and candour, and
in his heart, I am sure, valued him accordingly.  " I
have been twice married, Doctor," said Edwards,
apropos of nothing, cheerily adding the terrifying
sentiment, " You, I suppose, have never known
known what it was to have a wife? "  This—to
Johnson!  We can see Boswell shivering on his
chair's edge.  " Sir," said Dr. Johnson, " I have
known what it was to have a wife, and [in a solemn,
tender, faltering tone] I have known what it was
to lose a wife.  It had almost broke my heart."
Edwards was unabashed.  He said instantly, " How
do you live, sir? " adding, " For my part, I must
have my regular meals and a glass of good wine."
Dr. Johnson replied suitably—the kind of reply
that would usually settle the matter among his
guests—" I now drink no wine, sir.  Early in life
I drank wine;  for many years I drank none.  I
then for some years drank a great deal."  Edwards
rose to a fine height of irreverence here, to the
immense dismay, I have no doubt, of Boswell,
who, with all his advantages, had not been at
Pembroke with his hero.  He cut in with, " Some
hogsheads, I warrant you."  The Doctor succeeded
in taking no notice (quite possibly he was secretly
flattered;  we all like to be credited with great
deeds), and continued his dull alimentary history;

but the victory was Edwards's, for the Doctor, when asked if he ate supper, merely and very uncharacteristically said "No," leaving it for his visitor to remark, with something of the great man's own manner made human, "For my part, now, I consider supper as a turnpike through which one must pass in order to get to bed."

That is good enough; but it is not the single remark by which Edwards is known—on which his deathless fame rests. That had come earlier. "You are a philosopher, Dr. Johnson," said Edwards. "I have tried, too, in my time to be a philosopher; but I don't know how; cheerfulness was always breaking in." That was Edwards's great speech. By virtue of that candid confession he takes his place with the shining company of simple souls, the hierarchy of the ingenuous. It was too much for Boswell, who had no eye for children, young or old. But on repeating it to Mr. Burke, Sir Joshua Reynolds, Mr. Courtenay, Mr. Malone, and, indeed, all the eminent men he knew, they said with one accord that "it was an exquisite trait of character." He therefore refrained from belittling it in the book.

To Boswell's intense relief, Edwards at last went. He had begun by calling Dr. Johnson (who was sixty-nine) old; he left with another reference to his age. Looking him full in the face, he said, "You'll find in Dr. Young the line,

O my coevals! remnants of yourselves."

When he was gone, Boswell came to himself again,

and quickly remarked that he thought him a weak man; and the Doctor, smarting under the imputation of senility, was, I regret to say, weak enough to agree. But they were both wrong. Edwards was a strong man—strong in his cheerfulness and his transparency.

# THE DREAM CHILDREN OF LITERATURE

## By Richard Le Gallienne

There is a corner of the world of dreams filled with the voices of little children, as a wood is filled with the singing of birds. It is peopled with those "nurslings of immortality," who, with a divine precocity, have, as we say, made names for themselves no less personal and everlasting than those of some of their elders—children as typically "childish" as some great soldier is typically soldierly, or as Helen of Troy is typically womanly. There was no need for them to grow up to become immortal, for they live for ever just because they are always children—children, as one might say, who have supremely succeeded —as children.

Of all these it was Paul Dombey who, unconsciously enough, raised the banner of the child. Dickens is very near to Shakespeare in that moment of divination when the little frail and moonlit Paul is first taken to school and confronted with the magnificent Dr. Blimber—Dr. Blimber, who means so well in his plush, middle-class way.

" Shall we make a man of you ? " asked Dr. Blimber.

Little Paul replied: " I would rather be a child."

I would rather be a child!

Without knowing it, how right little Dombey was! Who is there amongst us that does not protest against growing up, does not battle against maturity, and does not try his best to remain a child? Who of us with any sense is anxious to grow up? Is it not always felt to be a special grace of nature when we say of anyone that he has kept the heart of a child? This we say of Goldsmith, of Lamb, and of Stevenson, with the sense of paying them signal tribute, and the first law of most greatness is the law of the Kingdom of Heaven.

To be made a man of by Dr. Blimber, or by those other disillusionising agencies of experience employed in licking our immortal beings into mortal shape, may be a very fine thing—but happy is he who has succeeded in remaining a child, has kept his heart pure, has escaped the pride and the cynicism of knowledge, and can still turn eyes of uncontaminated simplicity upon human life and all the wonder of the world.

Dream children!

When Lamb wrote that immortal fragment of his own pathos, he was thinking of two little children who might have been his, had he not through life remained a bachelor, for his sister's sake. He cheered his lonely evening thought with the fancy of taking little Alice and John on his knees, and telling them, paternal fashion, about the time when *he* was a child, till suddenly, as the story neared its end, the soul of the first Alice looked out of the eyes of the little dream Alice so poignantly that the dream was broken, and, as the children faded away, he seemed to hear them saying: " We are not of Alice, nor of thee, nor are we children at all. The children of Alice call Bartrum father. We are nothing; less than nothing, and dreams. We are only what might have been. . . ."

Perhaps others of us have personal dream children of this sort—the little boy that never came to us, or the little girl that went too early away, while she was still a mere snowdrop in February; but it is not of such dream children I would write, but rather of those who belong to the whole world's dreamland—that corner of the world of dreams where we may come upon a little girl in a red hood carrying dainties in her basket for an old grandmother who lives in a lonely hut in the forest, the same forest where you may find two babes lying asleep under a coverlet of leaves which the kind robins are spreading over them, or meet with Little Boy Blue blowing his horn, or come just in time to save Little Silverlocks from the three bears: there is no end to the famous people you may meet in this corner of the dream world, and so little is it necessary to grow up to become famous that one can seriously claim that there are no names better known than those one meets with there. Think of being as famous as

Little Red Riding-hood! Napoleon himself is hardly as well known as Goody Two-shoes! Adelina Patti is hardly more famous than Mr. Riley's "Little Orphant Annie"! Let us wander in this land awhile, and see if we can meet with any more of its famous inhabitants!

Yes; here comes Kilmeny, a Scotch maiden, with a strange dream on her face. For seven long years she has been missing from her home in the glen, and her home-folks mourn her as dead.

> Kilmeny, Kilmeny, where have you been?
> Lang hae we sought baith holt and den;
> By linn, by ford, and greenwood tree,
> Yet you are halesome and fair to see.
> Where gat you that joup [mantle] o' the lily sheen,
> That bonnie snood of the birk sae green?
> And these roses, the fairest that ever were seen?
> Kilmeny, Kilmeny, where have you been?

Kilmeny has been to fairyland, and here in the twilight she is coming back home to tell them about it all.

> Kilmeny looked up with a lovely grace,
> But nae smile was seen on Kilmeny's face;
> As still was her look and as still was her e'e,
> As the stillness that lay on the emerant lea,
> Or the mist that sleeps on a waveless sea.
> For Kilmeny had been, she knew not where,
> And Kilmeny had seen what she could not declare;
> Kilmeny had been where the cock never crew,
> Where the rain never fell, and the wind never blew.
> But it seemed as the harp of the sky had rung,
> And the airs of heaven played round her tongue,
> When she spake of the lovely forms she had seen,
> And a land where sin had never been;
> A land of love and a land of light,
> Withouten sun, or moon, or night;

Where the river swelled, a living stream,
And the light a pure celestial beam;
The land of vision, it would seem,
A still, an everlasting dream.

But she will stay only a little while, and then
wander back to fairyland. She was not of this
world, after all.

It wasna her hame, and she couldna remain;
She left this world of sorrow and pain,
And returned to the land of thought again.[1]

But here is a less eerie apparition—a merry
little fellow, without shoes or stockings, intent
on dabbling up and down the stream. He calls
himself "the barefoot boy," and, if you know
your poets, you will stroke his curly head and say:

Blessings on thee, little man,
Barefoot boy, with cheek of tan!
With thy turned-up pantaloons,
And thy merry whistled tunes;
With thy red lip, redder still
Kissed by strawberries on the hill;
With the sunshine on thy face,
Through thy torn brim's jaunty grace;
From my heart I give thee joy,—
I was once a barefoot boy. . . .

But before you have finished he will have
escaped into a treetop, and be whistling back to
the wood robins.

As he swings there, you will be reminded of a
similar apparition of elfish childhood from another

[1] The story of Kilmeny is, of course, told by James
Hogg, the Ettrick Shepherd, in the beautiful ballad from
which these lines are quotations.

12

land and another time—though yet, they say, still inhabiting ours. He carries a bow and arrows, and is even more scantily clad than our " barefoot boy." One of the most vivid descriptions I can find of him is this from an old Greek writer (Longus) who knew him well:

As I entered my garden to-day, about noon, I espied a little boy under my pomegranates and myrtles, some of which he had gathered; and he was holding them in his hands. His complexion was white as milk, his hair a bright yellow, and he shone as if he had just been bathing. He was naked and alone, and amused himself with plucking the fruit with as much freedom as if it had been his own garden. . . . I asked him to what neighbour he belonged, and what he meant by gathering what grew in another person's garden. He made no reply, but, approaching very near me, smiled sweetly in my face, and pelted me with myrtle berries, and (I know not how) so won upon me that my anger was appeased. I entreated him to come close to me, and assured him that I wished only to give him one kiss, for which he should ever after have liberty to gather as much fruit, and to pluck as many flowers as he pleased. Upon hearing me thus address him, he burst into a merry laugh, and replied:

" I am not the child I appear to be; but I am older than Saturn, ay, older than Time himself. I knew you well, Philetas, when you were in the flower of your youth, and when you tended your widely-scattered flock in yonder marsh. I was near you, when you sat beneath those beech trees, wooing your Amaryllis; I was close to the maiden, but you could not discern me. . . ." With these words he sprang like the youngling of a nightingale among the myrtles, and, climbing from bough to bough, ascended through the foliage to the summit of the tree. I observed wings upon his shoulders, and between them a tiny bow and arrows; but in a moment I could see neither him nor them.

This charming description is taken from *The Delectable History of Daphnis and Chloe*, that exquisite idyl of boy and girl love which may be called the *Paul and Virginia* of the ancient world; yet, if Daphnis and Chloe and Paul and Virginia are little more than children, they are, perhaps, too near to the frontier of grown-up romance to be classed among " dream children." Our dream children are, for the most part, in that earlier period when the opposite sex is an uncongenial rather than a congenial mystery—when the little girl is apt to regard the little boy as a disagreeable species of wild animal, and the little boy to wonder what little girls can possibly be good for. Of course, there are exceptions. Fred Vincy married little Mary Garth with a ring taken from an old umbrella stick, while they were still babies, and in actual life such infantine matrimony is not unusual; but, so far as I know, it has found no striking exponents in childhood romance. We must not forget, though, that Dante and Beatrice were only nine when they first met, and, if their story belongs rather to history, it is history so transformed into poetry that Dante's well-known description of his first beholding Beatrice may well go among our " dream pictures " :

. . . when first the glorious lady of my mind was made manifest to mine eyes, even she who was called Beatrice by many who know not wherefore, she had already been in this life for so long as that, within her time, the starry heaven had moved toward the eastern quarter one of the twelve parts of a degree; so that she appeared to me at the beginning of her ninth year almost, and I saw her almost at the end of my ninth year. Her dress, on that day, was of a most noble colour, a subdued and goodly crimson, girdled and adorned in such sort as best suited with her very tender age. At that moment, I say most truly, the spirit of life, which hath its dwelling in the secretest chamber of the heart, began to tremble so violently that the least pulses of my body shook therewith; and in trembling it said these words: *Ecce deus fortior me, qui, veniens, dominabitur mihi.* [Here is a deity stronger than I; who, coming, shall rule over me.]

Yet, as a rule, the dream children of fame seldom go in couples, though now and again we do meet them holding each other's hands for company in the mysterious wood of the world. Such a forlorn and fear-stricken pair, which the imaginative pity of centuries has long immortalised, are, of course, " the princes in the Tower," shapes of boyish helplessness in an evil world, which concentrate more dramatically than any others the piteous, lonely terror of children before the menace of the unknown evil of life. We have seen them in many pictures, stealing fearfully among the grim shadows of the wicked old stones, and has not Shakespeare shown them to us, in such a pity of innocent sleep that even their murderers turned poets as they slew them?

" Lo, thus," quoth Dighton, " lay those tender babes!"
" Thus, thus," quoth Forrest, " girdling one another
Within their innocent alabaster arms;

15

Their lips were four red roses on a stalk,
Which in their summer beauty kissed each other.
A book of prayers on their pillow lay
Which once," quoth Forrest, " almost changed my
     mind . . ."

While we are with Shakespeare, shall we not
look again on the little Arthur, and his keeper,
Hubert, another child shape lighting up like a
lily the dungeons of those bloody times—another
boy prince with " his little kingdom of a forced
grave "? But, before we return to the lonely
children, let us not forget a happier picture of a
famous two, that of St. Theresa and her little
brother setting out—the saintly mites—to seek
for martyrdom among the Moors!

However, as I said, the dream child is usually
met alone, and the fact may be taken as symbolic
of that pathetic isolation of childhood in a world
of grown-up mysteries for which even the kindest
mother somehow fails to give any adequate explanation. The child asks this question and that,
receives an answer no less puzzling than the original
mystery, and goes back again into his loneliness,
to ponder it out for himself. Perhaps no other
human being is so lonely as a thinking child.
Surrounded on every hand with the cabalistic
writing of the strange world into which he has
suddenly awakened, he asks himself, again and
again, why he is here, how he came, and what it
all means. Of course, no one can tell him, because
no one knows any more about it than himself—
but the grown-ups don't say that. They say that

he will understand it all when he grows up. They
mean that he will have ceased to ask questions,
found commonplace solutions, or given up expecting answers—as the shades of the prison-house
more and more darken around the eager little
beam of inquiry. Even a Whittier must cease to
be a barefoot boy, and even a Wordsworth, so
sensitive to the mystic harmonies of existence,
and so close a confidant of the soul of the world,
has sadly to confess thus that dimming of the
spiritual eye, that deadening of the spiritual ear,
which comes with the passing of youth:

> Heaven lies about us in our infancy!
> Shades of the prison house begin to close
>     Upon the growing boy,
> But he beholds the light, and whence it flows,
>     He sees it in his joy;
> The youth, who daily farther from the east
> Must travel, still is nature's priest,
>     And by the vision splendid
>     Is on his way attended;
> At length the man perceives it die away
> And fade into the light of common day.

Wordsworth was the first to give us the lonely
child in literature, and to say over the names of
such little heroines of his as Lucy Gray and Alice
Fell is to call up pictures of childhood almost
unbearably wistful with their penetrating sense
of solitariness.

> Oft I had heard of Lucy Gray;
>     And, when I crossed the wild,
> I chanced to see, at break of day,
>     The solitary child. . . .

How simple the lines are, but with what an
intense loneliness they fill the heart!—what a
poignant tenderness for the little figures so forlorn
there in all that wilderness of heath and sky!—
and, as the poem proceeds, surely the pathos of all
children that have ever lost their way and never
been seen again is concentrated in its broken-
hearted close.

How solitary, too, was that other Lucy whom
Wordsworth has immortalised thus:

> A maid whom there was none to praise,
>   And very few to love:
>
> A violet by a mossy stone,
>   Half hidden from the eye;
> Fair as a star, when only one
>   Is shining in the sky.

The little maid in "We are Seven" seemed
unconscious of her solitude, so sure was she that
her brothers and sisters were still with her, though
unseen; yet what a loneliness is there in the
verses, and what a pathos in the very faith with
which, at sunset, she brings her little porringer
into the churchyard, and eats her supper by the
graves of her lost playfellows. Again, how the
"Solitary Reaper" echoes with upland loneliness:

> Behold her, single in the field,
> Yon solitary Highland lass,
> Reaping and singing by herself! . . .

In other poets, children are usually represented
as romping and singing in happy bands at play;

they are unindividualised groups of joyous creatures, like clumps of primroses, or flocks of birds; but with Wordsworth, for whom, as we know, " the child is father to the man," theirs is already the loneliness of the individual, with the added isolation of a little creature " moving about in worlds not realised." They have the look on their faces of small travellers who have come a long journey, and find themselves set down in a strange land, and their hearts are lonely for the brighter land they have left. They always seem to be looking for the hidden road home again. That is the meaning of that wistful look upon their faces, and who knows but that, when, as we say, they lose their way in the snow, they have really found their way home?

With Dickens, the archcreator of dream children, it is, again, as with Wordsworth, always the lonely child, and with what a love did his great heart go out to the little beings his imagination has made immortal! What an almost divine pity he has for the fears and bewilderments and hardships of their dependent little lives, so at the mercy of grim elders, and the sport of all manner of heartless, bullying forces! Poor David Copperfield and that dreadful new father-in-law of his with the black whiskers—how one's blood runs cold for him as Mr. Murdstone takes him into a room and sternly expounds to him, in ogreish words, the iron discipline to be expected for breaches of the law in that sepulchral household! Children are not

beaten, nowadays, I am told. If not, the change
is largely due to Dickens, who has certainly done
much to mitigate the former severe lot of the child
—in a *régime* where the father was little more to
his children than the stern policeman and execu-
tioner of home, the dread Rhadamanthus in the
best parlour, who must on no account be disturbed
by childish laughter, and to offend whom was to
invite swift and certain doom.

How much has Dickens done to mitigate the
lot of the schoolboy by his savage satire of Dothe-
boy's Hall, and the lot of all poor boys whatsoever
by the pleading figure of Oliver Twist! There are
few strokes in literature so trenchant in their tragic
laughter, so irresistibly comic in their shattering
criticism of human nature, as that scene which
has passed into the proverbs of the world—the
scene, of course, where poor little starved Oliver
asks for more. The astonishment on the face of
the cook is positively Olympian in its humour.
A charity boy ask for more! Why, the very walls
of the institution rocked, and the earth quaked,
at such a request, and the rumour of it passed
like thunder from room to room, till even the
board of directors, then in session, must have
heard it. Great heavens! " Oliver Twist has
asked for more."

Again, the pity of the lot of frail and sick
children foredoomed to death from their cradles,
who else has ever made it touch the heart
like Dickens, with Paul Dombey and Tiny Tim?

There are no children in the world of dreams whose faces we know better than these: Paul, with his air of only paying life a rather weary little visit, having to go soon, and brave little Tim, who, for all his crutches and irons, would sing his tiny song—a song, though, " about a lost child travelling in the snow "—and give his cheerful toast with the rest at the Christmas dinner.

How like Dickens it was to put that " God bless us, every one! " into the mouth of a little cripple that was soon to die. Yes; there are many little graves in Dickens's volumes, and on no other graves in the world, perhaps, have so many tears been shed.

So at length we come to Little Nell—the queen of all the dream children. We meet her often in that world of dreams, from the moment when she first looks up at us in the street, a self-possessed, but " just a little frightened " wisp of a child, and begs us to tell her the way home to her grandfather's, to the moment when she lies silent and smiling among the winter berries and green leaves she had loved. " When I die," she had said, " put near me something that has loved the light, and had the sky above it always." So there she lies among the berries and the green leaves.

" You do well to speak softly," says her old grandfather. " We will not wake her. I should be glad to see her eyes again, and to see her smile. There is a smile upon her young face now, but it is fixed and changeless. I would have it come and go. That shall be in Heaven's good time. We will not wake her."

Nell, too, belongs to the little lonely ones—but surely her grave is not lonely.

Another lonely child we shall often meet in our corner of the world of dreams is Maggie Tulliver, much communing with her earnest young soul " of God and nature and of human life," and carrying in her hand an old thumbed copy of *The Imitation of Christ.* No one else has understood so well as George Eliot the thoughtful religious child, and portrayed the spiritual agonies of the young with so intimate a knowledge; and, incidentally, one may add that no other writer has described with such painful reality and delightful humour the sufferings of such children from prosaic and grotesque relations.

Another dream child, too, belongs to her— the child that Silas Marner found on his hearthstone, one winter evening, whose shining curls he at first mistook for his stolen gold come back to him again; " but, instead of the hard coin with the familiar resisting outline, his fingers encountered soft warm curls," the gold that was to soften, not harden, his heart.

At the thought of bright babes that soften the hearts of strong men, there flashes on the eye across the centuries the very different picture in which Homer makes us behold great Hector, all dreadfully girt in his war-harness, taking his little son in his arms before going into battle—little

Astyanax, " like unto a beautiful star." But the child, " dismayed at his dear father's aspect, in dread at the bronze, and at the horsehair crest that he beheld nodding fiercely from the helmet's top," shrinks from him and cries for his nurse, and Hector and Andromache laugh together, and the father takes off the dreadful headgear, so that the child is no longer afraid, and, tossing him in his arms, prays aloud to Zeus that old human prayer —so seldom answered—that he may become a better man than his father!

To somersault back again through time, we must not forget our little friend Alice, the type of all lonely children who " make up things " out of the wonderland of their fancy, and, being so lonely, make friends of the very furniture, and fairy tales even out of sofas—like the boy in Stevenson's " child's garden." It would be ungrateful to forget such still older friends as Sandford and Merton, Tom Brown, and the boy who has stood so long upon the burning deck. Then there are the naughty children like Budge and Toddy, the impish boys like Flibbertigibbet in *Kenilworth*, and the gentle children who make goodness almost as fascinating as naughtiness, such as Timothy of the Quest and Little Lord Fauntleroy.

I said that the dream children seldom go in couples, but you may sometimes meet them in companies and groups. One eager company you may meet at the heels of a wizard piper playing the sweetest of strange tunes—but here again is a lonely child, the Tiny Tim of mediæval legend, the little lame boy who couldn't keep up with his companions, and came to the fairy hill just too late, only in time to catch a glimpse of its shining inside and hear the great doors close on all the music.

Then there is the rosy group of children that pulled at Charlotte's skirts while she was cutting bread, and made Werther think that she never before looked so charming as when surrounded by all this chubby clamour.

There are, doubtless, other groups of children one might think of, but there is one group of all we cannot forget, that sacred little group that years ago in Judea brought down so tender a blessing upon all children.

Dream children ! Yes! if we grown-ups are such stuff as dreams are made of—what must the children be?

# MARIA EDGEWORTH

## By Brander Matthews

MARIA EDGEWORTH was born on the first day of January, 1767; and she died on the twenty-second of May, 1849. There were granted to her more than eighty-two years of useful and happy life.

In her fourscore years she was a silent witness of the American revolution, of the French revolution, of the rise and fall of Napoleon, and of the suppressed revolts of 1848. She saw the beginnings of the romanticist movement in literature, and she survived to behold the solid foundation of modern realism laid by Balzac. In the year of her birth, Sterne published the ninth and final volume of *Tristram Shandy*; and in the year of her death, Dickens began to issue *David Copperfield* and Thackeray to send forth the successive parts of *Pendennis*. She was a living bridge from the eighteenth century to the nineteenth. It was a tumultuous spectacle that passed before her serene gaze; and she looked at this shifting panorama of human life with shrewd understanding and humorous toleration, as keenly interested at the end as she had been at the beginning.

Her father, Richard Lovell Edgeworth (born

in 1744 and dying in 1817), was a man of remarkable individuality. He was the owner of a large estate in Ireland, at Edgeworthstown, and his ownership extended over Pallasmore (where Goldsmith had been born in 1728). Mr. Edgeworth was inventive, but too far in advance of his time to see his suggestions adopted in his own lifetime. He had early been taken captive by Rousseau's theories on education as set forth in *Emile*; and he still commands respect as an early educational reformer in England. He was a member of the Irish parliament which voted the Union; and it was characteristic of his intellectual independence that, after making a speech in favour of the Union, he unexpectedly voted against it— an act which perhaps cost him a peerage. He was an admirable landlord, beloved by his tenants, toward whom he was as firm as he was encouraging. Near the end of his life he declared that he was not a man of prejudices: " I have had four wives. The second and third were sisters, and I was in love with the second in the lifetime of the first." By these four wives he had nineteen children, thereby supplying himself with abundant material for the practice of his principles of education.

Maria was the eldest child, the first of the four he had by his first wife. She resided with her aunts until her mother's death. Four months later her father married the beautiful Honora Sneyd, with whom he had long been in love; and he then took his bride and children over to

Ireland, where his home was to be for the rest of his long life. He had had a Welsh ancestress, from whom Maria may have derived something of her Celtic imaginative sympathy, as she may have inherited her turn for sentiment from her mother, who was German by descent. She was only six or seven when she was first taken to Ireland; and although she was sent to school in England for a little while when the family had to return to England temporarily because of the failing health of the second Mrs. Edgeworth, she went back to Ireland again in 1782, when she was only fifteen, after her father had buried Honora Sneyd and married a sister, Elizabeth, at the request of the dying Honora.

It was in her impressionable youth that Maria Edgeworth gained her intimate acquaintance with Ireland and with the Irish; and it is in the memories of this plastic period that she was to find the material for those later stories which now keep her name alive. Her father employed her to write his business letters; and he had her with him when he received his tenants and listened to their pleas.

Many of the masterpieces of fiction are the direct result of this utilisation of youthful experiences unconsciously assimilated. The *David Copperfield* of Dickens, the *Pendennis* of Thackeray, the *Huckleberry Finn* of Mark Twain, have all of them the richness of tone and the accent of veracity which are evident also in *Castle Rackrent* and in

27

*The Absentee.* Maria Edgeworth was to transmute
into fiction her father's theories of education,
and she was to win fleeting success as a novelist
of fashionable life in London; but it is by her
imaginative reproduction of Irish character, sus-
tained by this early intimacy and vivified by
enduring appreciation, that she has established
her fame upon its solid foundation. The didacticism
which vitiates *The Parent's Assistant* is no longer
tolerable, and the society which is mirrored in
*Ormond* and *Helen* and *Belinda* has lost its interest
for us, now that the kaleidoscope of life has
turned and turned again. But *Castle Rackrent*
and *The Absentee* abide; they are not only tales
with an unfading charm, but also human documents
of unimpaired value.

As the eldest daughter, Maria became her
father's unfailing companion, looking up to him
with equal affection and admiration, feelings
which he repaid with interest. She lived on terms
of loving friendship with her succession of step-
mothers; and she helped them to mother the
swarming brood of brothers and sisters which
were the result of Mr. Edgeworth's four marriages.
She early revealed herself to be what she always
remained, sympathetic and sensible, fun-loving
and unpretentious, free from all affectation, and
ready always to lend a helping hand. Her earlier
tales were composed to amuse the family, with
little or no thought of publication. Often they were
first written on a slate, to be copied out in ink

only when they had won the approval of the household.

It was not until 1795, when she was twenty-eight, that she published her first book, *Letters to Literary Ladies*, a plea for the education of women, inspired by her father, who was in advance of his time in urging that the opportunity for culture should be offered to girls as well as to boys. Three years later, *Practical Education* was issued with the names of both the father and the daughter on the title page. This ill-digested but suggestive book, with its digressions and its didacticism, may be regarded as the first fruit of that long collaboration in authorship, which was, as the daughter declared, "for so many years the joy and pride of my life." The partnership seems to have been advantageous when Maria helped her father, but it revealed itself as far less useful when he chipped and corrected and pulled about his daughter's work, forcing it arbitrarily to conform to his theories, and injecting deliberate morality into what might otherwise have been a pure work of art. Perhaps the only time when this literary partnership justified itself completely, was in the delightful *Essay on Irish Bulls* which the father and the daughter composed in 1802.

After Miss Edgeworth had once "tasted ink," and after she had savoured the pleasure of popular appreciation, the pen was rarely allowed to fall from her hand; and for nearly two-score years she proved herself to be possessed of that abundant productivity which is evidence of literary affluence. *Castle Rackrent* was issued in 1800 without her name, although this was disclosed in the second edition which followed at no long interval. A year later she put forth a collection of *Moral Tales*, to which her father contributed a needless and needlessly inflated preface. It was followed in the same year (1801) by the first of her longer novels of fashionable life, *Belinda*, a story now dropping out of memory, like most of her other tales of social ambition and of social achievement.

After the peace of Amiens the whole family went over to France; and it was in Paris in 1803, when she was thirty-six, that she fell in love. Her wooer was a Swede, Edel Cranz, who felt that he had no right to give up his duty to his own king. Maria, on her part, could not face the separation from her father and from the happy family of which she was the most devoted member. The lovers parted for ever; and Maria did not find it easy to regain her habitual good spirits. She went back to Ireland, and she returned to her writing. Perhaps it was fortunate for her just then that she carried on all her literary labours, the composition of her books as well as the conduct of her abundant correspondence, not in the seclusion of her own study, but in the general sitting-room, with the ample bevy of children playing all about her. And in the next few years she wrote half-a-dozen volumes. It was in the *Popular Tales*, which was sent forth in 1812, that she published one of the best of her briefer Irish stories, *Rosanna*; and it was in a second series of *Tales of Fashionable Life*, issued in that same year, 1812, that she published *The Absentee*, the longest of these Irish studies.

She was now one of the best known figures of a brilliant literary period; and when she paid a visit to London in 1813 she was most warmly received —although her father failed to win an equal liking. He died in 1817, to the abiding grief of his loyal daughter, who dutifully completed the memoirs he had left behind him. In 1823 she went to Edinburgh to see Sir Walter Scott; and in 1825 Scott crossed over to Ireland to return the visit. It was in 1829 that Scott wrote the general preface to the Waverley Novels, in which he declared that "without being so presumptuous as to hope to emulate the rich humour, pathetic tenderness, and admirable tact" with which Miss Edgeworth had represented Irish character, he had felt that something might be attempted for Scotland of the same kind which she had "so fortunately achieved for Ireland." To the unpretending and innately modest author of *Castle Rackrent*, probably this tribute was as surprising as it was grateful.

She retained to the end of her life her interest in ideas, in things, and in persons—especially in persons. The gift for friendship survived unimpaired to the end; and she had attained almost to threescore years and ten when she received a visit from George Ticknor and his wife, who won their way immediately into her affection and to whom many of the pleasantest of her later letters are addressed. When she was almost eighty she was a spectator of all the miseries of the famine of 1846; and, despite her many years, she was untiring in her efforts to relieve the distress which she saw all about her. Three years later she passed away, having survived almost to the end of the first half of the nineteenth century. Her chief competitor in the same branch of fiction, Jane Austen, born in 1775, eight years later, had died in 1817, thirty-two years earlier, after a life little more than half as long as hers.

It would be doing a disservice to Maria Edgeworth to set her up as a rival of the incomparable Jane Austen. She had not the mastery of construction, the all-pervasive humour, the absolute certainty of touch; she was rarely the impeccable artist in character-delineation which Miss Austen nearly always is. She is less deliberately and resolutely artistic; and she is likely to be more wilfully didactic, as though she had less confidence in the intelligence of her readers. And as a result, *Helen*, *Belinda*, and *Ormond* are now fading pictures of a vanished social era, while the colours of *Pride and Prejudice* and of *Sense and Sensibility* are as fresh as ever. But if Miss Edgeworth is inferior to Miss Austen in form and in finish, in the exquisite delicacy of execution, she was perhaps on two or three occasions more fortunate in her choice of theme, and in the material out of which she wove her fictions. The undeniable limitation of Miss Austen's work for the readers of to-day is to be discovered in its narrowness, in its hardness—if this word is not too harsh—in its complacent acceptance of a scheme of life, of a social order, which seems to many of us not only remote but pitiably empty and offensively pretentious. Of course, human nature is unendingly interesting; and it is human nature that Miss Austen catches in the act; but her men and her women dwell in a very special world, with a very restricted outlook on life, and even her dexterity, her personal charm, her omnipresent humour cannot make this portrayal of a civilisation now happily extinct for ever appealing to a majority of readers of this twentieth century of ours. Our point of view is no longer that taken by Miss Austen, and we are often revolted by things which she accepted tranquilly. This may be a misfortune for us as well as for her; but nevertheless it is a fact.

It is only when she is content to be an artist, and not a moralist, that Miss Edgeworth is really a rival of Miss Austen; and it is only when she deals with Irish life and character that she puts forth her full power. Her tales of fashionable life have been superseded; what she therein attempted has been more successfully achieved by others —especially by Thackeray, who was born in the year when she published *The Absentee*. The various stories of child-life, contained in *The Parent's Assistant* and in other volumes, are still readable, but they are vitiated by over didacticism, by a strenuous insistence upon the obvious moral— an insistence which sometimes warps the conduct of the tale. Stevenson revealed his customary shrewdness when he declared that morality is often wantonly thrust into English fiction, "like a carpet thrown over a railing." We are now coming to a wider conception of the purpose of fiction, and we prefer a morality which stiffens the story like the backbone in man, and which is not stuck in like a pin through a butterfly, to use an apt illustration of Hawthorne's.

Miss Edgeworth herself seems to have been naturally an artist, but she yielded to parental pressure. Mr. Edgeworth would have resented and denounced Lord Morley's assertion that "it is a commonplace to the wise, and an everlasting puzzle to the foolish, that direct inculcation of morals should invariably prove so powerless an instrument, so futile a method. The truth is that nothing can be more powerfully efficacious from the moral point of view than the exercise of an exalted creative art, stirring within the intelligence of the spectator active thought and curiosity about many types of character and many changeful issues of conduct and fortune; at once enlarging and elevating the range of his reflections on mankind, even kindling his sympathies into the warm and continuous glow which glorifies and strengthens nature, and fills men with that love of humanity which is the best inspirer of virtue."

If proof were needed of the futility of the direct inculcation of morals it could be found in the failure of the various tales in *The Parent's Assistant* to retain the interest of the young folks for whose moral guidance they were written. And if proof were needed of the abiding value, from the moral point of view, of " the exercise of an exalted creative art " which can kindle our sympathy and enlarge the range of our reflections, it can be found in *Castle Rackrent* and in *The Absentee*. In these twin-masterpieces Miss Edgeworth was content to let character speak for itself, and to relinquish to the story itself the duty of pointing its moral. In these tales she escaped from the unfortunate influence of her father; and she followed in the footsteps of Cervantes and Shakespeare and Molière; she attains to something of their large detachment and disinterestedness. She conveyed the impression of life itself; and every reader is free to draw his own conclusions and to discover for himself the significance of the scenes which have been displayed before his eyes.

*Castle Rackrent* is apparently the first in point of time of all Irish stories; and to this day it remains the first in point of merit. Lover and Lever and Carleton may have imitated it and emulated it; but they were none of them able to surpass it. It is a masterpiece which even Miss Edgeworth herself never surpassed; so Mrs.

Ritchie has declared " the little volume contains the history of a nation." In less than a hundred pages she has sounded the depths of the Irish character which she knew so well and appreciated so keenly. She makes us see for ourselves the wit and the humour of the Irish, their shortsightedness and their irresponsibility, their clannishness and their loyalty. She sets before us the Irish as they are—or at least as they were in the final years of the eighteenth century. She shows us the racial characteristics actually at work. Her method is very modern in its unflinching realism; but veracious as this realism is, searching as it is, it is never harsh or hostile. It is with love and with loving kindness that she evokes these native types and sets them in motion before us, so that they may reveal themselves amply and unhesitatingly.

She is essentially sympathetic in her understanding of the peasants and of the gentry she is portraying with invincible fidelity. Never does she assume an attitude of superiority, of condescension, or even of aloofness. And here she is to be sharply distinguished from the later French realists, Flaubert especially, not to speak of Zola, who seem to be dissecting, with what must be described as callous disregard, inferior creatures, never caring to conceal their shallow contempt for the objects of their chilly inquest. Miss Edgeworth is wholly free from this inhuman remoteness. She may make us laugh at the strange beings who people these Irish tales; but she makes us like them also, and feel sorry for them at the very moment when we see them reaping what they have sown. She had not only a feminine felicity of observation and a feminine subtlety of insight into motive, she had also a womanly warm-heartedness. Scott hit on Miss Edgeworth's primary quality when he declared that in writing the Waverley Novels he had wished to attempt for Scotland what she had done for Ireland, "something which might introduce her natives to those of the sister kingdom in a more favourable light than they had been placed hitherto, and tend to procure sympathy for their virtues and indulgence for their foibles." And Scott succeeded in this attempt, partly because he himself possessed what Mrs. Ritchie has asserted to be Miss Edgeworth's special quality, a gift " for perceiving through the minds of others, and for realising the value of what they in turn reflected; one is struck again and again by the odd mixture of intuition and of absolute matter of fact which one finds in her writings "—and in Scott's also.

What makes *Castle Rackrent* more interesting than Miss Edgeworth's other Irish stories is its greater simplicity of structure, and its utilisation of the artistic device of transparency, of that ironic presentation which permits the reader to peer behind the external statement and to interpret this in his own fashion. It is Thady, the devoted retainer, who tells us all about the successive owners of Castle Rackrent, and he is never sparing of praise; and yet we see through his assertions and beyond them, and we swiftly come to our own opinion of these masters of his, an opinion diametrically opposed to that proclaimed by the faithful eulogist of the family. This device of transparency, possibly suggested to Miss Edgeworth by Fielding, was borrowed from her by Thackeray for the autobiography of Barry Lyndon, that marvellous scoundrel who is for ever boasting of his virtues. And Miss Edgeworth is less afraid for the success of this device than Thackeray, or else she is less doubtful of the intelligence of her readers, for she never descends to the explanatory footnote which "gives the whole thing away," if so plebeian a phrase may be permitted here. Thackeray knew Miss Edgeworth's Irish stories well and relished them highly; and it was in an early essay of his, *On a Box of Novels*, that he dwelt on the underlying melancholy of Irish fiction; "from *Castle Rackrent* downward, every Hibernian tale that I have read is sure to leave a sort of woeful tender impression."

*The Absentee* is inferior only to *Castle Rackrent*, and perhaps only because it lacks a Thady for its narrator. In a footnote to his history Macaulay testified to the veracity of this story, and to the importance of one figure in it as a revelation of racial characteristics; and elsewhere he went so far as to compare the last scene in the story to an episode in the *Odyssey*. Mrs. Ritchie has recorded how she once heard Ruskin break out in praise and admiration of the book; "you can learn more of Irish politics by reading it than from a thousand columns out of blue-books." Possibly a part of the vivacity and of the swift movement of *The Absentee* is to be ascribed to the fact that it was originally composed as a play— like Thackeray's *Lovel the Widower* and Charles Reade's *Peg Woffington*. Although it is ever dangerous to try to make a play out of a novel, it is always easy and often advantageous to make a novel out of a play. It may be noted also that the manager to whom the comedy was submitted was Richard Brinsley Sheridan, himself an Irishman and the creator of that most charming of all stage-Irishmen, Sir Lucius O'Trigger. Sheridan was well equipped to appreciate the humour and the truth of Miss Edgeworth's only dramatic effort; but he was also a practical politician, and he felt sure that, in the existing condition of politics, the Lord Chamberlain would refuse the licence needed before the piece could be performed.

There is one inexorable test by which we can gauge the abiding value of an author's work; this is the measuring of the range and of the depth of the influence it has exerted upon later writers. Excepting only the great masters of fiction— with whom Miss Edgeworth need not be classed— few can withstand this test as triumphantly as she does. Scott was proud to acknowledge that he had followed in her footsteps; and Cooper, who trod the trail blazed by Scott, owed her a

debt at least for Betty Flanagan in *The Spy*—
a humorous character which Miss Edgeworth
cordially appreciated, declaring that "it could
not have been better drawn by an Irish pen."
Lover and Lever, Carleton and Banim, cultivated
the field she had first planted, and ploughed with
her heifer. Thackeray borrowed more than one
hint from *Castle Rackrent* for use in *Barry Lyndon*,
which is perhaps the most vigorously artistic
of all his stories. Nor was her influence confined
to writers of her own tongue. Turgenief, for
example, is on record with the confession that it
was her treatment of the Irish peasantry which
first opened his eyes to the possibility of a similar
presentation of the Russian labourer; and the
*Memoirs of a Sportsman* was the exciting cause
of the abolition of serfdom.

Sooner or later, no doubt, some novelist would
surely have been moved to deal sympathetically
with life among the lowly, since it was impossible
that fiction should always maintain its early
attitude of aristocratic condescension toward the
plain people. Yet it is to Miss Edgeworth's everlasting credit that it was she who was actually
the first to renounce this remote superiority,
and to take a truly democratic view of the despised tillers of the soil, bringing these humble
folks, too long ignored, within the radius of
appreciative understanding.

# TALES OF THE SEA

## By Joseph Conrad

It is by his irresistible power to reach the adventurous side in the character, not only of his own, but of all nations, that Marryat is largely human. He is the enslaver of youth, not by the literary artifices of presentation, but by the natural glamour of his own temperament. To his young heroes the beginning of life is a splendid and warlike lark, ending at last in inheritance and marriage. His novels are not the outcome of his art, but of his character, like the deeds that make up his record of naval service. To the artist his work is interesting as a completely successful expression of an unartistic nature. It is absolutely amazing to us, as the disclosure of the spirit animating the stirring time when the nineteenth century was young. There is an air of fable about it. Its loss would be irreparable, like the curtailment of national story or the loss of an historical document. It is the beginning and the embodiment of an inspiring tradition.

To this writer of the sea the sea was not an element. It was a stage, where was displayed an exhibition of valour, and of such achievement as the world had never seen before. The greatness of that achievement cannot be pronounced imaginary, since its reality has affected the destinies of nations; nevertheless, in its grandeur it has all the remoteness of an ideal. History preserves the skeleton of facts and, here and there, a figure or a name; but it is in Marryat's novels that we find the mass of the nameless, that we see them in the flesh, that we obtain a glimpse of the everyday life and an insight into the spirit animating the crowd of obscure men who knew how to build for their country such a shining monument of memories.

Marryat is really a writer of the Service. What sets him apart is his fidelity. His pen serves his country as well as did his professional skill and his renowned courage. His figures move about between water and sky, and the water and the sky are there only to frame the deeds of the Service. His novels, like amphibious creatures, live on the sea and frequent the shore, where they flounder deplorably. The loves and the hates of his boys are as primitive as their virtues and their vices. His women, from the beautiful Agnes to the witch-like mother of Lieutenant Vanslyperken, are, with the exception of the sailors' wives, like the shadows of what has never been. His Silvas, his Ribieras, his Shriftens, his Delmars remind us of people we have heard of somewhere, many times, without ever believing in their existence. His morality is honourable and conventional.

There is cruelty in his fun and he can invent puns in the midst of carnage. His naïveties are perpetrated in a lurid light. There is an endless variety of types, all surface, with hard edges, with memorable eccentricities of outline, with a childish and heroic effect in the drawing. They do not belong to life; they belong exclusively to the Service. And yet they live; there is a truth in them, the truth of their time; a headlong, reckless audacity, an intimacy with violence, an unthinking fearlessness, and an exuberance of vitality which only years of war and victories can give. His adventures are enthralling; the rapidity of his action fascinates; his method is crude, his sentimentality, obviously incidental, is often factitious. His greatness is undeniable.

It is undeniable. To a multitude of readers the navy of to-day is Marryat's navy still. He has created a priceless legend. If he be not immortal, yet he will last long enough for the highest ambition, because he has dealt manfully with an inspiring phase in the history of that Service on which the life of his country depends. The tradition of the great past he has fixed in his pages will be cherished for ever as the guarantee of the future. He loved his country first, the Service next, the sea perhaps not at all. But the sea loved him without reserve. It gave him his professional distinction and his author's fame—a fame such as not often falls to the lot of a true artist.

At the same time, on the other side of the

Atlantic, another man wrote of the sea with true artistic instinct. He is not invincibly young and heroic; he is mature and human, though for him also the stress of adventure and endeavour must end fatally in inheritance and marriage. For James Fenimore Cooper nature was not the framework, it was an essential part of existence. He could hear its voice, he could understand its silence, and he could interpret both for us in his prose with all that felicity and sureness of effect that belong to a poetical conception alone. His fame, as wide but less brilliant than that of his contemporary, rests mostly on a novel which is not of the sea. But he loved the sea and looked at it with consummate understanding. In his sea tales the sea interpenetrates with life; it is in a subtle way a factor in the problem of existence, and, for all its greatness, it is always in touch with the men, who, bound on errands of war or gain, traverse its immense solitudes. His descriptions have the magistral ampleness of a gesture indicating the sweep of a vast horizon. They embrace the colours of sunset, the peace of starlight, the aspects of calm and storm, the great loneliness of the waters, the stillness of watchful coasts, and the alert readiness which marks men who live face to face with the promise and the menace of the sea.

He knows the men and he knows the sea. His method may be often faulty, but his art is genuine. The truth is within him. The road to legitimate realism is through poetical feeling, and he pos-

sesses that—only it is expressed in the leisurely
manner of his time. He has the knowledge of
simple hearts. Long Tom Coffin is a monumental
seaman with the individuality of life and the
significance of a type. It is hard to believe that
Manual and Borroughcliffe, Mr. Marble of Marble-
Head, Captain Tuck of the packet-ship *Montauk*,
or Daggett, the tenacious commander of the *Sea
Lion* of Martha's Vineyard, must pass away some
day and be utterly forgotten. His sympathy is
large, and his humour is as genuine—and as
perfectly unaffected—as is his art. In certain
passages he reaches, very simply, the heights of
inspired vision.

He wrote before the great American language
was born, and he wrote as well as any novelist of
his time. If he pitches upon episodes redounding
to the glory of the young republic, surely England
has glory enough to forgive him, for the sake of his
excellence, the patriotic bias at her expense. The
interest of his tales is convincing and unflagging;
and there runs through his work a steady vein of
friendliness for the old country which the succeed-
ing generations of his compatriots have replaced
by a less definite sentiment.

Perhaps no two authors of fiction influenced so
many lives and gave to so many the initial impulse
towards a glorious or a useful career. Through
the distances of space and time those two men of
another race have shaped also the life of the writer
of this appreciation. Life is life, and art is art—

and truth is hard to find in either. Yet in testimony to the achievement of both these authors it may be said that, in the case of the writer at least, the youthful glamour, the headlong vitality of the one and the profound sympathy, the artistic insight of the other—to which he had surrendered—have withstood the brutal shock of facts and the wear of laborious years. He has never regretted his surrender.

# THE GREY KIRK

## By R. B. Cunninghame Graham

In a grey valley between hills, shut out from all the world by mist and moors, there lies a village with a little church.

The ruined castle in the reedy loch, by which stand herons fishing in the rank growth of flags, of bulrush and hemp-agrimony which fringes it, is scarcely greyer than the hills. The outcrop of the stone is grey, the louring clouds, the slated roofs, the shingly river's bed and the clear water of the stream. The very trout that dart between the stones, or hang suspended where the current joins the linn, look grey as eels.

Green markings on the moors show where once paths the border prickers followed on their wiry nags led towards the south, the land of fatted beeves and well-stored larders, clearly designed by Providence or fate to be the jackman's prey, but long disused, forgotten and grassed over, though with the ineffaceable imprint of immemorial use still clear.

Dark, geometrical plantations of black fir and spruce deface the hills, which nature evidently made to bear a coat of scrubby oak and birch.

Wire fences gird them round, the posts well tarred
against the weather, and the barbed wire so taut
that the fierce winds might use them as Æolian
harps, could they but lend themselves to song.

A district which the wildness of the past has
so impressed, that the main line of railway steals
through its corries and across its moors as it were
under protest, and where the curlew mocks the
engine's whistle with his wilder cry.

The village clusters round the kirk, as bees
crowd round their queen, the older houses thatched.
Their coping-stones carved with a rope, remain to
show how, in the older world, their rustic architects
secured their roofs against the blast.

No doubt the hamlet grew between the castle
and the church. The jackman of the chief, the
sacristan and kindly tenants of the church, ready
and near at hand to put on splent and spur, and
able to take lance or sprig of hyssop in their hand
at the first tinkle of the bell or rout of horn.

The castle in the loch has dwindled to a pile
of stones, from which spring alders, birches and
sycamores, whose keys hang yellow in the wind,
unlocking nothing but the sadness of the heart,
which marks their growth, from the decay of the
abandoned keep.

A modern mansion set with its shrubberies and
paltry planted woods, where once the Caledonian
forest sheltered the wild white cattle in its glades,
seems out of place in the surrounding grey. Its
lodge, with trim-cut laurels and with aucubas and

iron gate, run in a foundry from a mould, is trivial, comfortable and modern; and the low sullen hills appear to scorn it in their fight with time, for they remain unchanged from the bold time of rugging and of rieving, when spearsmen, not a pensioned butler, kept the gate.

The crumbling and decayed stone wall, secluding jealously the boggy meadows of the park, shuts off the modern mansion with its electric light, its motor-cars, its liveried servants and its air of castellated meanness, from the old houses huddling in the wynd. They look towards the chapel with its high-pitched roof, its squat round tower with crenellated top and its sharp windows pointed like a lance. It seems to gaze at them, as if it felt they were the only links that time has left it with its own old world. The eye avoids the modern buildings in the town, the parish church, four-square and hideous, with windows like a house, and from the hills falls on the chapel and is satisfied. Only in some old missal, with the illustrations by some monk adscribed to his small round of daily cares, can you behold its equal, as it stands desolate and grey.

The chapel of a race of warriors, men dark and grey as is the stone of which its walls are built, once a lone outpost of the great mother fort in Rome, it lingers after them, sheltering their tombs and speaking of their fame. Instinctively one feels that once its doors stood open, just as it were a mosque or church in lands where faith continues the whole week, and men pray as they eat or sleep, just when they feel inclined, and naturally as birds.

In the green churchyard, whose grassy hillocks wave it like a sea, the long grey tombstones of the undistinguished dead appear like boats that make towards some haven, laying their courses by the beacon of the tower.

The church itself floats like a ship turned bottom upwards on the grassy sea. Its voyage is ended, and the men who once clattered in armour in its aisles and through its nave now sleep below its flags. A maiméd ritual and a sterner creed prevail, and those who worship in the church have shown their faith by laying down encaustic tiles over the spur-marked stones on which their forbears jingled in their mail. A fair communion table of hewn stone, smug and well-finished and with the wounds upon the bleeding heart all stanched (as one would think), stands where the altar stood, cold and uninteresting, a symbol of the age. *Non ragioniam;* on every side, lie those who, in their time, carried their wars across the border, and on the bridge at Rome charged on the people who pressed round them, just as they would have charged in Edinburgh, had any other clan presumed to take the croon of the old causeway of the High Street, and brought upon themselves an excommunication from the Pope.

Stretched under canopies of stone they lie,

looking so grim and so impenitent, that one is sure they must be satisfied with their presentments, if, looking down on their old haunts, they see their images. Many are absent who would have filled a niche right worthily, Tineman and the Black Knight of Jedburgh and others of the house, who, in their time, shook Scotland to the core. But in the middle of the aisle, in leaden caskets hooped with iron and padlocked, lie two hearts. One, that of Archibald who belled the cat. The other heart has travelled much, and in its life beat higher with all generous thoughts than any of its race.

He who possessed it (or was possessed by it), liked ever better, as he said, to hear the laverocks' singing than the cheeping of the mouse. His hands were able, all his adventurous life, to keep his cheeks from scars, as he averred in Seville to the Spanish knight, who wondered at their absence from his face. Carrying a heart to Palestine, he fell, not in the Holy Land, but on the frontiers of Granada, that last outpost of the Eastern world. The heart he carried lies at Melrose, and his own, sealed fast in lead, soldered perhaps in some wild camp lost in the Ajaráfé of Sevilla, is the chief ornament of the grey chapel of his race.

Set like a ship, the chapel lies in the long waves of sullen hill and moor that roll away towards the south.

In its long voyage through the sea of time,

crews of wild warriors have clung to it, as their one refuge from the spear of life. Each in their turn have fallen away, leaving it lonely, but still weather-tight and taut; a monument of faith, as some may think, or of good masonry and well-slaked lime, as the profane may say, still sailing on the billowy moors which stretch towards Muir-kirk; so little altered that any one of those who in the past have prayed within its walls, if he returned to a changed world, would cling to it as the one thing he knew.

So it drifts on upon its voyage through time, bearing its freight of warriors to their port.

# ON AN UNKNOWN COUNTRY

## By Hilaire Belloc

TEN years ago, I think, or perhaps a little less or perhaps a little more, I came in the Euston Road —that thoroughfare of Empire—upon a young man a little younger than myself whom I knew, though I did not know him very well. It was drizzling and the second-hand booksellers (who are rare in this thoroughfare) were beginning to put out the waterproof covers over their wares. This disturbed my acquaintance, because he was engaged upon buying a cheap book that should really satisfy him.

Now this was difficult, for he had no hobby, and the book which should satisfy him must be one that should describe or summon up, or, it is better to say, hint at—or, the theologians would say, reveal, or the Platonists would say *recall*—the Unknown Country, which he thought was his very home.

I had known his habit of seeking such books for two years, and had half wondered at it and half sympathised. It was an appetite partly satisfied by almost any work that brought to him the vision of a place in the mind which he had always intensely desired, but to which, as he had then long guessed, and as he is now quite certain, no human paths directly lead. He would buy with avidity travels to the moon and to the planets, from the most worthless to the best. He loved Utopias and did not disregard even so prosaic a category as books of real travel, so long as by exaggeration or by a glamour in the style they gave him a full draught of that drug which he desired. Whether this satisfaction the young man sought was a satisfaction in illusion (I have used the word " drug " with hesitation), or whether it was, as he persistently maintained, the satisfaction of a memory, or whether it was, as I am often tempted to think, the satisfaction of a thirst which will ultimately be quenched in every human soul I cannot tell. Whatever it was, he sought it with more than the appetite with which a hungry man seeks food. He sought it with something that was not hunger but passion.

That evening he found a book.

It is well known that men purchase with difficulty second-hand books upon the stalls, and that in some mysterious way the sellers of these books are content to provide a kind of library for the poorer and more eager of the public, and a library admirable in this, that it is accessible upon every shelf and exposes a man to no control, except that he must not steal, and even in this it is nothing but the force of public law that interferes. My friend therefore would in the natural course of things have dipped into the book and left it there;

but a better luck persuaded him. Whether it was
the beginning of the rain or a sudden loneliness in
such terrible weather and in such a terrible town,
compelling him to seek a more permanent com-
panionship with another mind, or whether it was
my sudden arrival and shame lest his poverty
should appear in his refusing to buy the book—
whatever it was, he bought that same. And since
he bought the Book I also have known it and have
found in it, as he did, the most complete expression that I know of the Unknown Country, of
which he was a citizen—oddly a citizen, as I then
thought, wisely as I now conceive.

All that can best be expressed in words should
be expressed in verse, but verse is a slow thing to
create; nay, it is not really created: it is a
secretion of the mind, it is a pearl that gathers
round some irritant and slowly expresses the very
essence of beauty and of desire that has lain long,
potential and unexpressed, in the mind of the
man who secretes it. God knows that this Unknown Country has been hit off in verse a hundred
times. If I were perfectly sure of my accents I
would quote two lines from the *Odyssey* in which
the Unknown Country stands out as clear as does
a sudden vision from a mountain ridge when the
mist lifts after a long climb and one sees beneath
one an unexpected and glorious land; such a
vision as greets a man when he comes over the
Saldeu into the simple and secluded Republic of
the Andorrans. Then, again, the Germans in their

idioms have flashed it out, I am assured, for I remember a woman telling me that there was a song by Schiller which exactly gave the revelation of which I speak. In English, thank Heaven, emotion of this kind, emotion necessary to the life of the soul, is very abundantly furnished. As, who does not know the lines:

> Blessed with that which is not in the word
> Of man nor his conception: Blessed Land!

Then there is also the whole group of glimpses which Shakespeare amused himself by scattering as might a man who had a great oak chest full of jewels and who now and then, out of kindly fun, poured out a handful and gave them to his guests. I quote from memory, but I think certain of the lines run more or less like this:

> Look how the dawn in russet mantle clad
> Stands on the steep of yon high eastern hill.

And again:

> Night's candles are burnt out, and jocund day
> Stands tiptoe on the misty mountain tops.

Which moves me to digress. . . . How on earth did any living man pull it off as well as that? I remember arguing with a man who very genuinely thought the talent of Shakespeare was exaggerated in public opinion, and discovering at the end of a long wrangle that he was not considering Shakespeare as a poet. But as a poet, then, how on earth did he manage it?

Keats did it continually, especially in the

*Hyperion.* Milton does it so well in the Fourth Book of *Paradise Lost* that I defy any man of a sane understanding to read the whole of that book before going to bed and not to wake up next morning as though he had been on a journey. William Morris does it, especially in the verses about a prayer over the corn; and as for Virgil, the poet Virgil, he does it continually like a man whose very trade it is. Who does not remember the swimmer who saw Italy from the top of the wave?

Here also let me digress. How do the poets do it? (I do not mean where do they get their power, as I was asking just now of Shakespeare, but how do the words, simple or complex, produce that effect?) Very often there is not any adjective, sometimes not any qualification at all: often only one subject with its predicate and its statement and its object. There is never any detail of description, but the scene rises, more vivid in colour, more exact in outline, more wonderful in influence, than anything we can see with our eyes, except perhaps those things we see in the few moments of intense emotion which come to us, we know not whence, and expand out into completion and into manhood.

Catullus does it. He does it so powerfully in the opening lines of

*Vesper adest . . .*

that a man reads the first couplet of that Hymeneal, and immediately perceives the Apennines.

The nameless translator of the Highland song

does it, especially when he advances that battering
line:

And we in dreams behold the Hebrides.

They all do it, bless their hearts, the poets, which
leads me back again to the mournful reflection
that it cannot be done in prose. . . .

Little friends, my readers, I wish it could be
done in prose, for if it could, and if I knew
how to do it, I would here present to you that
Unknown Country in such a fashion that every
landscape which you should see henceforth could
be transformed, by the appearing through it,
the shining and uplifting through it, of the Unknown Country upon which reposes this tedious
and repetitive world.

Now you may say to me that prose can do it,
and you may quote to me the end of the *Pilgrim's
Progress*, a very remarkable piece of writing. Or,
better still, as we shall be more agreed upon it,
the general impression left upon the mind by the
book which set me writing—Mr. Hudson's *Crystal
Age*. I do not deny that prose can do it, but when
it does do it, it is hardly to be called prose, for it
is inspired. Note carefully the passages in which
the trick is worked in prose (for instance, in the
story of Ruth in the Bible, where it is done with
complete success), you will perceive an incantation
and a spell. Indeed this same episode of Ruth in
exile has inspired two splendid passages of European verse, of which it is difficult to say which is
the more national, and therefore the greatest,

Victor Hugo's in the *Légende des Siècles* or Keats's
astounding four lines.

．　　　．　　　．　　　．　　　．　　　．

There was a shepherd the other day up at
Findon Fair who had come from the east by
Lewes with sheep, and who had in his eyes that
reminiscence of horizons which makes the eyes of
shepherds and of mountaineers different from the
eyes of other men. He was occupied when I came
upon him in pulling Mr. Fulton's sheep by one
hind leg so that they should go the way they were
desired to go. It happened that day that Mr.
Fulton's sheep were not sold, and the shepherd
went driving them back through Findon Village,
and up on to the high Downs. I went with him
to hear what he had to say, for shepherds talk
quite differently from other men. And when we
came on to the shoulder of Chanctonbury and
looked down upon the Weald, which stretched
out like the Plains of Heaven, he said to me: " I
never come here but it seems like a different place
down below, and as though it were not the place
where I have gone afoot with sheep under the
hills. It seems different when you are looking
down at it." He added that he had never known
why. Then I knew that he, like myself, was perpetually in perception of the Unknown Country,
and I was very pleased. But we did not say anything more to each other about it until we got
down into Steyning. There we drank together

and we still said nothing more about it, so that to this day all we know of the matter is what we knew when we started, and what you knew when I began to write this, and what you are now no further informed upon, namely, that there is an Unknown Country lying beneath the places that we know, and appearing only in moments of revelation.

Whether we shall reach this country at last or whether we shall not, it is impossible to determine.

# ON THE APPROACH OF AN AWFUL DOOM

## By Hilaire Belloc

My dear little Anglo-Saxons, Celt-Iberians and Teutonico-Latin oddities—The time has come to convey, impart and make known to you the dreadful conclusions and horrible prognostications that flow, happen, deduce, derive and are drawn from the truly abominable conditions of the social medium in which you and I and all poor devils are most fatally and surely bound to draw out our miserable existence.

Note, I say " existence " and not " existences." Why do I say " existence," and not " existences " ? Why, with a fine handsome plural ready to hand, do I wind you up and turn you off, so to speak, with a piffling little singular not fit for a half-starved newspaper fellow, let alone a fine, full-fledged, intellectual and well-read vegetarian and teetotaller who writes in the reviews ? Eh ? Why I say " existence " ?—speaking of many, several and various persons as though they had but one mystic, combined and corporate personality such as Rousseau (a fig for the Genevese!) portrayed in his *Contrat Social* (which you have never read), and such as Hobbes, in his *Leviathan* (which some of you have heard of), ought to have premised but did not, having the mind of a lame, halting and ill-furnished clockmaker, and a blight on him!

Why now " existence " and not " existences "? You may wonder; you may ask yourselves one to another mutually round the tea-table putting it as a problem or riddle. You may make a game of it, or use it for gambling, or say it suddenly as a catch for your acquaintances when they come up from the suburbs. It is a very pretty question and would have been excellently debated by Thomas Aquinas in the Jacobins of St. Jacques, near the Parloir aux Bourgeois, by the gate of the University; by Albertus Magnus in the Cordeliers, hard by the College of Bourgoyne; by Pic de la Mirandole, who lived I care not a rap where and debated I know not from Adam how or when; by Lord Bacon, who took more bribes in a day than you and I could compass in a dozen years; by Spinoza, a good worker of glass lenses, but a philosopher whom I have never read nor will; by Coleridge when he was not talking about himself nor taking some filthy drug; by John Pilkington Smith, of Norwood, Drysalter, who has, I hear, been lately horribly bitten by the metaphysic; and by a crowd of others.

But that's all by the way. Let them debate that will, for it leads nowhere unless indeed there be sharp revelation, positive declaration and very certain affirmation to go upon by way of Basis or First Principle whence to deduce some sure conclusion and irrefragable truth; for thus the intellect walks, as it were, along a high road, whereas by all other ways it is lurching and stumbling and boggling and tumbling in I know not what mists and brambles of the great bare, murky twilight and marshy hillside of philosophy, where I also wandered when I was a fool and unoccupied and lacking exercise for the mind, but from whence, by the grace of St. Anthony of Miranella and other patrons of mine, I have very happily extricated myself. And here I am in the parlour of the "Bugle" at Yarmouth, by a Christian fire, having but lately come off the sea and writing this for the edification and confirmation of honest souls.

What, then, of the question, *Quid de querendo? Quantum? Qualiter? Ubi? Cur? Quid? Quando? Quomodo? Quum? Sive an non?*

Ah! There you have it. For note you, all these interrogative categories must be met, faced, resolved and answered exactly—or you have no more knowledge of the matter than the *Times* has of economics or the King of the Belgians of thorough-bass. Yea, if you miss, overlook, neglect, or shirk by reason of fatigue or indolence, so much as one tittle of these several aspects of a question you might as well leave it altogether alone and give up analysis for selling stock, as did the Professor of Verbalism in the University of Adelaide to the vast solace and enrichment of his family.

For by the neglect of but one of these final and

63

fundamental approaches to the full knowledge of
a question the world has been irreparably, irre-
trievably and permanently robbed of the certain
reply to, and left ever in the most disastrous
doubt upon, this most important and necessary
matter—namely, *whether real existence can be
predicated of matter.*

For Anaxagoras of Syracuse, that was tutor to
the Tyrant Machion, being in search upon this
question for a matter of seventy-two years, four
months, three days and a few odd hours and
minutes, did, in extreme old age, as he was walking
by the shore of the sea, hit, as it were in a flash,
upon six of the seven answers, and was able in
one moment, after so much delay and vexatious
argument for and against with himself, to resolve
the problem upon the points of *how, why, when,
where, how much,* and *in what,* matter might or
might not be real, and was upon the very nick of
settling the last little point—namely, *sive an non*
(that is, whether it *were* real or no)—when, as luck
would have it, or rather, as his own beastly appetite
and senile greed would have it, he broke off sharp
at hearing the dinner-gong or bell, or horn, or
whatever it was—for upon these matters the King
was indifferent (*de minimis non curat rex*), and so
am I—and was poisoned even as he sat at table
by the agents of Pyrrhus.

By this accident, by this mere failure upon *one*
of the Seven Answers, it has been since that day
never properly decided whether or no this true

existence was or was not predicable of matter; and some believing matter to be there have treated it pompously and given it reverence and adored it in a thousand merry ways, but others being confident it was not there have starved and fallen off edges and banged their heads against corners and come plump against high walls; nor can either party convince the other, nor can the doubts of either be laid to rest, nor shall it from now to the Day of Doom be established whether there is a Matter or is none; though many learned men have given up their lives to it, including Professor Britton, who so despaired of an issue that he drowned himself in the Cam only last Wednesday. But what care I for him or any other Don?

So there we are and an answer must be found, but upon my soul I forget to what it hangs, though I know well there was some question propounded at the beginning of this for which I cared a trifle at the time of asking it and you I hope not at all. Let it go the way of all questions, I beg of you, for I am very little inclined to seek and hunt through all the heap that I have been tearing through this last hour with Pegasus curvetting and prancing and flapping his wings to the danger of my seat and of the cities and fields below me.

Come, come, there's enough for one bout, and too much for some. No good ever came of argument and dialectic, for these breed only angry gestures and gusty disputes (*de gustibus non dis-*

*putandum*) and the ruin of friendships and the very fruitful pullulation of Dictionaries, textbooks and wicked men, not to speak of Intellectuals, Newspapers, Libraries, Debating-clubs, bankruptcies, madness, *Petitiones elenchi* and ills innumerable.

I say live and let live; and now I think of it there was something at the beginning and title of this that dealt with a warning to ward you off a danger of some kind that terrified me not a little when I sat down to write, and that was, if I remember right, that a friend had told me how he had read in a book that the damnable Brute CAPITAL was about to swallow us all up and make slaves of us and that there was no way out of it, seeing that it was fixed, settled and grounded in economics, not to speak of the precession of the Equinox, the Horoscope of Trismegistus, and *Old Moore's Almanack*. Oh! Run, run! The Rich are upon us! Help! Their hot breath is on our necks! What jaws! What jaws!

Well, what must be must be, and what will be will be, and if the Rich are upon us with great open jaws and having power to enslave all by the very fatal process of unalterable laws and at the bidding of Blind Fate as she is expounded by her prophets who live on milk and newspapers and do woundily talk Jew Socialism all day long; yet is it proved by the same intellectual certitude and irrefragable method that we shall not be caught before the year 1938 at the earliest and with luck we may run ten years more: why then let us make the best of the time we have, and sail, ride, travel, write, drink, sing and all be friends together; and do you go about doing good to the utmost of your power, as I heartily hope you will, though from your faces I doubt it hugely. A blessing I wish you all.

# MISS MARY WILKINS

## By W. L. COURTNEY

### I

THERE are few of our modern writers who have the art of the short story so much at their finger-ends as Miss Mary E. Wilkins. To talk of the technique of a particular author or authoress always strikes one with a chilling sense of pedantry. Nevertheless, there is no other way of describing Miss Wilkins's mastery over her materials than to say that she has, consciously or unconsciously, elaborated a perfect technique. Unconsciously probably, or almost certainly. For questions of technique, like questions of grammar, only arise after the good work of literature has been done. This is what makes the position of the grammarian or the critic useful, it may be, but hardly dignified. Neither one nor the other can lay down in advance the ideal types or forms which a living language or art is bound inevitably to assume. The artist does his work first, inventing his own technique as he goes along, and then, *longo intervallo*, comes the precise and analytic critic to point out the rules which underlie the new species, to dissect the structure, not in its breathing and living grace, but as one might put a pin through a butterfly in order to study its wings. The critic has to wait on the movements of genius, and is only whipper-in to the lame dogs of literature.

Miss Wilkins's stories illustrate very different kinds of excellence in their respective styles. A great many people, apparently, have not discovered how different in their essence are a short story and a novel. There must be always something pictorial in the short story. Its art is bound to be some variety of impressionism. Think of the conditions. Within thirty, forty, or fifty pages you have to convey to the reader a perfectly distinct and self-centred narrative, idea, or impression. You may do it by the suggestiveness which sets the reader's mind thinking, so that he can carry out and complete for himself the thing which you have hinted as a silhouette. Or else the author possesses one clear, masterful, and obvious idea, and sacrifices all the ordinary complexity of human nature in order to give it adequate illustration. In the first instance, you have what is in reality concentrated and essential history. In the second, you have a fragment of character, a specific trait or quality of human nature, the illumination of a temperament. Take, for instance, in Miss Wilkins's volume, *Silence*, a story which she calls " A New England Prophet." She is describing how a certain community in the Far West was suddenly seized and shaken by the not unfamiliar form of religious mania which believes that the world is at once coming to an end. In the Lennox farmhouse there is a collection of men and women transported out of their ordinary selves, mainly because Soloman Lennox seems to them an inspired seer, and Alonso Lennox, his son, fourteen years old, and deaf and dumb from his birth, draws wonderful pictures of flying angels on his slate. Here are materials out of which could be made a characteristic study of New England super-stition done in the form of an essay, or a detailed history of a peculiar phase of civilisation elaborated in a novel. But for Miss Wilkins's purposes the treatment must be different. As a short story it must be confined to one issue, the temporary madness of a New England prophet—just one phase of a gloomy and superstitious character. Soloman Lennox, with his denunciations and his parrot-cries of repentance, and his faith in the inspiration of his half-idiot son, is the centre of the picture. For the sake of contrast, there are grouped round him his easily persuaded wife, his half-shrinking daughter, Melissa, and an ironical and sceptical brother, Simeon Lennox, to serve as the vindication of common sense. Infatuated men and women make for themselves white flying garments to ascend into the air. They meet on the appointed evening on a neighbouring hill, and come back, wretched, bedraggled, dis-illusioned, in the morning. But Soloman Lennox, with his one over-mastering idea, gives the key-note of the whole, so that the last thing we see and remember is his shrunken figure, "sitting sadly within himself, a prophet brooding over the ashes of his own prophetic fire."

Take another example of the manipulation of the short story, where the great point is not to illustrate a phase of character, but to describe, with vivid and poignant touches, a scene. The first tale, "Silence," is a wonderful bit of impressionist art, where literature is so used as to become akin to painting, giving all the effect of colour and light and shade. Silence Hoit is the heroine, with a deep passionate love for David Walcott. Miss Wilkins never misleads us as to what she is trying to do. It is not the enduring love of maid and man with which she is occupying herself. That is only the excuse for the narrative. From the outset we are transported into a tense, nervous, electrical atmosphere, in the midst of which the village of Deerfield is feverishly expecting a midnight attack by the Indians and the French. "'Oh, David! what is that on your cloak? What is it?' David looked curiously at his cloak. 'I see naught on my cloak save old weather-stains,' said he. 'What mean you, Silence?' Silence quieted down suddenly. 'It is gone now,' said she, in a subdued voice. 'What did you see, Silence?' Silence turned towards him; her face quivered convulsively. 'I saw a blotch of blood,' she cried; 'I have been seeing them everywhere all day. I have seen them on the snow as I came along.'" There it is, on the second page of the story, a vague, thrilling impression of coming disaster, of which Silence is the mouthpiece. We know what to expect—all the terror of the midnight attack, the women who lose their reason and babble of green fields, the unmarried girl who frantically nourishes a dead baby, the storm of bloodshed and rapine which sweeps over the doomed village, the wives who are rigid and cold upstairs, the men with their grimy and blood-besprinkled faces firing madly into the dark. Silence is herself swept along the resistless current of fate. Her lover is torn away from her as a prisoner, and only after many days returns to her arms. But nothing matters, nothing concerns us, save this lurid picture of a frontier village, smiling in peace and prosperity one day and a ruined mass of smouldering beams and horribly mutilated corpses the next morning.

There are other varieties of the short story which are not nearly so successful as these two. You can have a condensed history, like that which is called " The Buckley Lady," where a poor, patient little girl, endowed with a beautiful face, is educated to expect a lordly lover who never comes, and after many years is run away with by a man of her own choice. Or, again, " Evelina's Garden," dealing with two generations of Evelinas, the second representative of the name reproducing not only the features, but also the fate of the first, though with a difference. The condensed history never makes quite so good a short tale as the impressionist variety. Or, again, you may have a mere passing fancy like " Lydia Hersey of East Bridgewater," who makes the discovery that for a woman really to love a man she must first be dominated by him. Or, once again, belonging to the same *genre*, an imaginative fantasy, with something symbolic in it, like " The Little Maid at the Door," in which the poor, piteous figure of the deserted child of parents charged with witch-craft stands for I know not what of humanity and mercy and loving-kindness at death-grips with the stern cruelty of religious persecution. The last is, of course, a common form with many writers. Maeterlinck affords an obvious example in those little dramatic sketches where each phase and action is nothing in itself, but exists as a symbol of imaginative mysticism. D'Annunzio, too, has tried the same effect in his *Sogno d'un Mattino di Primavera*, the little drama acted by Eleonora Duse, in which the heroine, with her wits shattered by a horrible scene of bloodshed, learns a new sense of mystical communion and sympathy with Nature's operations—the rise of the sap in the tree, the growth of leaves, the bursting of buds. But, if I am not mistaken, the real progenitor of Miss Wilkins is Nathaniel Hawthorne. If there ever was a man who under-stood the conditions of the short story it was the author of *Mosses from an Old Manse*, possessing in far greater measure than Miss Wilkins, but using, in much the same spirit, the singular power of suggesting a great deal more than he says. Some day Miss Wilkins may be able to write stories like " The Birthmark," " Young Goodman Brown," and " Rappacini's Daughter." She has not done so yet, but she is inspired by the same ideals and appears to be capable of similarly delicate and exquisite workmanship.

## II

Miss Mary Wilkins may paint on a small canvas, but she is undoubtedly a true artist. From the simple and quiet truthfulness of *A New England Nun* we advance to the firm psychological drawing in *Pembroke*, and thence to the dramatic strength and vigour of *Madelon*. Miss Wilkins does not disturb the reader with many concurrent threads of narrative, nor does she crowd her scenes with subordinate characters; everything in her novel is dominated by the central conception of the heroine whose fate we watch with all the more interest because our attention is not distracted by the accessaries of the drama. Indeed, it may be said that the whole of her story is Madelon and nothing else—with a picturesque background formed by a New England winter, which accords with her stormy character far better than that burst of spring tenderness and summer warmth with which the authoress closes her narrative. Madelon is so strong, so passionate, so wild an animal that she seems only to touch the fringes of the world of human social life, and in her case domestic felicity and the ordinary joys and sorrows of wifehood and motherhood appear utterly out of place.

There is much in her ancestry which explains Miss Wilkins's heroine. Madelon Hautville, together with her father and her four brothers, belongs to a wholly different order of life from that which is usually found among the Puritans of New England. The Hautvilles were said to have French and Indian blood in their veins—although it was far back in history, since the first Hautville, who, report said, was of a noble French family, had espoused an Iroquois Indian girl.

" The sturdy males of the family had handed down the name and the characteristics of the races through years of intermarriage with the English settlers. All the Hautvilles—the father, the four sons, and the daughter—were tall and dark, and straight as arrows, and they all had wondrous grace of manner, which abashed and half offended, while it charmed, the stiff village people. Not a young man in the village, no matter how finely attired in city-made clothing, had the courtly air of these Hautville sons in their rude half-woodland garb. Not a girl, not even Dorothy Fair, could wear a gown of brocade with the grace, inherited from a far-away French grandmother, with which Madelon wore indigo cotton."

Let us add that the whole family were as musical as a band of troubadours, which made them at once popular and despised. David Hautville, the father, played the bass viol, Louis was a master of the violin, Eugène sang a sonorous tenor, Abner and the youngest son, Richard, contributed bass and treble respectively; while Madelon stood in the midst of her relations with her marvellous soprano voice dominating the entire harmony. The picture of this strange family is drawn with no little vigour and skill. Strangers and foreigners they remained in a land which half feared them, equipped as they were with abnormal qualities so alien to the commonplace nature of their surroundings.

No one could imagine that Madelon's life was likely under such circumstances to run through smooth channels. At the outset of the tale there are two men who love her, two cousins, Burr Gordon and Lot Gordon, essentially dissimilar in character, just as they differed also in natural strength and beauty. Lot Gordon is more or less of an invalid, with a subtle concentrated nature of his own, incapable of inspiring affection, but for that very reason, perhaps, bountifully endowed with a wonderful power of loving. Burr Gordon is the lighter hearted, more athletic, more inconstant swain, easily led away to flirt with the prim little Puritan girl, Dorothy Fair, while it is only Madelon who can touch the deeper fibres of his being. There is no particular cordiality, of course, between the cousins—all the more because Lot has the money and Burr the good looks, because the former loves and the latter is loved. But Madelon is not one who can deviate from her appointed path through any chance vacillations of sentiment or feeling; her devotion admits of no change or abatement, and when Burr Gordon, at a village ball, dances with Dorothy Fair rather than with herself, all the wilder characteristics derived from her Indian ancestors burst into acute and energetic life. And now comes the crisis of the story. Leaving the ballroom with mad pulses beating in her veins, she meets in the darkness of her homeward path a man, whom she supposes to be her faithless lover, but who is in reality Lot Gordon, and in a sudden burst of frenzy stabs him in the side. Burr Gordon comes up at the moment, and, in order to screen her from the consequences of the crime, sends her home, while he himself remains by the body of his wounded rival. The notorious jealousy of the cousins affords an easy explanation to the villages of the real meaning of the tragedy, and while Lot Gordon is taken to his house to recover slowly and painfully of his wound, Burr is hurried to prison in order to stand his trial for an attempted murder. It is from this point that the ceaseless energy and devotion of Madelon begins to assert itself with overwhelming force. She will not allow herself to suppose that the man in prison loves her as she loves him, but nothing must be left undone to rescue him from his undeserved fate, and bring the proper punishment on her own head.

From Lot Gordon she can obtain no single word which will help her; he lies in his bed and refuses to speak, lest the true explanation of the case should bring harm on Madelon. But there are other things to be done to set things straight. Madelon hurries to her rival, Dorothy Fair, and drags her, with or without her consent, to see Burr Gordon in prison, under the hope that he may at least confess to the Puritan girl that he was guiltless of the deed. When this, too, fails— for the captive knows how to keep his secret— Madelon walks ten miles in the midst of a terrible frost to one of the guests at the ball, who, she hopes, can help her in explaining her sole responsibility for the crime. This walk of ten miles is a marvel of descriptive force—one of the passages which stamps Miss Wilkins as an accomplished delineator of New England nature.

" The pasture lands were hummocked with ice-coated rocks and hooped with frozen bines; they seemed to flow down in glittering waves, like glaciers, over the hillsides. The woods stood white and petrified, as woods might have done in a glacial era. There was no sound in them, except now and then the crack of a bough under the weight of ice and slow, painful responses, like the twangs of musty harp-strings to the harder gusts of wind. The cold was so intense that the ice did not melt in the noonday sun, and there were no soft droppings and gurglings to modify this white rigour of light and sound. Occasionally a rabbit

crossed Madelon's path, silent as a little grey
scudding shadow, and so swiftly that he did not
reach one's consciousness until he was out of sight."

Nothing can quell Madelon's fiery vigour, even
when this painful journey fails to bring her the
evidence she requires. Without stint or stay, she
still works hard for the incarcerated man—albeit
that she says to herself that he loves not her, but
Dorothy Fair. At last she makes Lot Gordon
speak, by that sheer impetuosity of hers which
can take no denial; but he will only consent, on
the condition that Madelon marries him, to assert
that his own hand had struck the blow. At all
events, this confession will save Burr Gordon,
and that is all that Madelon cares about. Other
things may take their course if only he be saved.

Up to this point we have a firm and consistent
portraiture; but it is difficult to imagine how Miss
Wilkins could have brought herself to suppose
that either poetic justice or psychology required
a happy ending for this imbroglio. Madelon,
the wild creature of the woods, was, of course,
only half civilised, and she would have been better
placed in the older time, when her forefathers
hunted through the snow, or broke the ice on the
river for fish. The staid and primitive order of a
New England village weighed too heavily on her
spirits; she could not tune her character to the
commonplace melodies which sufficed for Puritan
girls like Dorothy Fair. But for this very reason
Nature and life were bound to be hard on her;

we cannot fancy her either as a wife or mother. Nevertheless the authoress makes, in the long run, everything come right, to the wonted sound of marriage bells. When the moment arrives for the performance of her promise, Lot Gordon releases Madelon from her word, Dorothy Fair suddenly shows a partiality for Eugène Hautville and relinquishes Burr for her rival; and even when Lot Gordon's wound threatens to burst out afresh, and so imperil the dawning happiness of Madelon, the wounded man chooses to turn his own hands against his life, and thus leave no doubt behind him as to how he died. All this patching of frayed and broken threads, this healing of discords and difficulties with more or less commonplace expedients, serve only to dim and darken the original portrait of Madelon. Pictured as she was, she could never have gained the trivial and normal happiness of the girls and boys around her. She belonged to another stock, and bore within her a different destiny. Perhaps Miss Wilkins's design is to bring out the character of Lot Gordon, and to prove that in his case the essence of a perfected love is self-sacrifice. Certainly his character grows in strength and intensity as the novel progresses, but in the same proportion Madelon's seems to grow weaker. She is only at her best and truest when, maddened with despair and without one thought for herself, she is daring every expedient to save the man in prison, to prove to an unbelieving world that she is a wilful murderess, and to release from unjust constraint Burr Gordon—not that he might wed her, but be united with Dorothy Fair. This is the original Madelon, with her fiery unregulated instincts, her passionate love, her unwavering strength and devotion; and even if she had died in all her ancestral savagery, the reader might have felt more content than to see her at the end of the tale linking her life with a man in every sense unworthy of her, and transferring the crown of self-sacrifice from her own brows to those of the suicide, Lot Gordon.

### III

We have already said that Miss Mary Wilkins is an artist. But it still remains to specify the kind and quality of the work which she can do so well, the limits within which her powers are exercised, the particular range of her capacity. *The Portion of Labour*—which, with all respect to the great American public, we prefer to spell in our insular way—is very significant in this regard, for it is one of the longest, in some respects one of the finest, in other respects one of the least satisfactory of all the novels she has written. It is exceedingly long, not so much in the mere matter of pages, although these count up to as many as 563, but because of the irritating slowness of the development. Many of the chapters are little works of art in themselves, each occupied with a specific incident elaborated with consummate care. But the total result is disappointing, because at the end it seems like a collection of small stories, an amalgamation of carefully written episodes. The sense of proportion, which is one of the instinctive gifts of the artist, is wanting here; the reader cannot get hold of the main incidents, because every incident seems to occupy a front place in the picture. It is the old difficulty that you cannot realise the pattern because of the finely finished detail, that you cannot see the wood for the trees. Miss Wilkins is a great artist, but she is not an artist of the big canvas. Her skill is that of a Meissonier, and no amount of little Meissoniers can resemble a decorative tableau by Puvis de Chavannes.

In what sense, then, is *The Portion of Labour* one of the finest of her works ? Primarily, no doubt, because it is inspired by a serious purpose, or, to speak more accurately, it is occupied with a sombre, gigantic, impressive theme. Here and there the authoress lets us see what is in her mind in all these five hundred odd pages. We have it indicated in the very last page. The world is a working world, the man who does no work has no place, no right to exist. More than that, labour is not an end in itself, nor can we easily reckon its value by putting down to its credit the various magnificent successes it has been able to accomplish. Doubtless labour accomplishes the tasks of the world, just as from another and a lower standpoint it helps to accumulate the silver and gold, which, in their turn, provide fresh opportunities for labour. So, too, work adds to the sum of human happiness and love; but that, again, is an extraneous, an alien end. The real justification for a world in which labour is the principal element is the development of character. No man can touch work and be unaltered. He becomes better or worse, higher or lower, according to the temperament that is in him. Nor from this point of view can we make any distinction between different kinds of work. All labour has a dignity of its own, dependent not upon itself, but upon its reactions on the mind of the labourer. The material element counts for nothing; it is the spirit that quickeneth.

That is one of the main topics of the book before us, not obtrusively set forth, but only to be gathered in retrospect when we have waded through all the sixty-one chapters. And there is no better illustration of it than the scene when the little heroine, Ellen Brewster, who has the opportunity of going to college and educating herself, decides, for the sake of her father and her home, that she will become a humble operative in a shoe factory. The passage is wrought as carefully as is all Miss Wilkins's work.

" Ellen laughed. ' I'm not scared,' said she. Then they entered the factory, humming with machinery, and a sensation which she had not anticipated was over her. Scared she was not; she was fairly exultant. All at once she entered a vast room in which eager men were already at the machines with frantic zeal, as if they were driving Labour herself. When she felt the vibration of the floor under her feet, when she saw people spring to their stations of toil, as if springing to guns in a battle, she realised the might and grandeur of it all. Suddenly it seemed to her that the greatest thing in the whole world was work, and that this was one of the greatest forms of work—to cover the feet of progress of the traveller of the earth from the cradle to the grave. She saw that these great factories, and the strength of this army of the sons and daughters of toil, made possible the advance of civilisation itself, which cannot go barefoot. She realised all at once and for ever the dignity of labour, this girl of the people with a brain which enabled her to overlook the heads of the rank and file of which she herself formed a part. She never again, whatever her regret might have been for another life for which she was better fitted, which her taste preferred, had any sense of ignominy in this. She never again felt that she was too good for her labour, for labour had revealed itself to her like a goddess behind a sordid veil. Abby and Maria looked at her wonderingly; no other girl had ever entered Lloyd's with such a look on her face."

The heroine herself is one of the most elaborate pieces of portraiture in these pages. The character is built up with an infinity of little touches.

We see her first in her New England home, a sensitive, dreamy child, who runs away because she felt that she was an incumbrance rather than a help to her parents. For some days she remained in the house of Cynthia Lennox, who loved her with a fierce maternal instinct, a thwarted love to which Destiny had denied any natural outlet. Even after Ellen Brewster has run away once more to her own house, Cynthia remains her constant friend, and it is she who is anxious to send the girl to college, where there might be some scope for her ability. But Ellen lives amid very humble surroundings. Her father, Andrew, gets more and more incapable of work as the years go on; her mother and her aunt represent lower, more sordid types than that which belonged to herself; the thousand worries and agonies of a life passed in debt and poverty crowd upon the girl's intelligence, and yet help to educate her and bring out all that is noble and self-denying in her nature. Then love comes in her way, first the boyish love of Granville Toy, afterwards the more mature affection of Robert Lloyd, considerably above Ellen's station in life—one, in fact, of the proprietors who manage the big factory of the town. Meanwhile Ellen, working at her manual toil, seeing before her every day the hard, fierce grind of the labourer, his ceaseless toil, his scanty rewards, enlists herself heart and soul on the side of the operative against his employer. Here is an added difficulty in her path, for although her heart goes out in innocent affectionateness to Robert Lloyd, her instincts and her intellectual sympathies are wholly with the class amongst which she lives. It all comes right in the end, but only after much tribulation and anguish of spirit. Both Robert Lloyd and Ellen Brewster learn a great deal of the worth and honesty of their respective attitudes towards modern industrial problems. There is no solution suggested of the everlasting quarrel between capital and labour, except so far as a quick sympathy and instinctive helpfulness serve to smooth all such antagonisms. It is something for Ellen to learn the responsibilities of the employer; it is much more for Robert to appreciate the dignity and self-respect of the worker.

Thus we discover a second reason why *The Portion of Labour* is a fine piece of work. It is so because of the scrupulous care spent over the development of the characters. The book is a gallery of portraits, each of them with those distinctive marks which make them real and vital. Apart from Ellen and Robert, there is the Brewster household—Andrew, the patient, loving, inefficient father; Fanny, the mother; Eva, the aunt, with the tragedy of her life history; and the cold, rigid upright grandmother, appropriately called Mrs. Zelotes Brewster. Cynthia Lennox has been already mentioned, but there are also Norman Lloyd and his wife, and Lyman Risley—an incisive little sketch of a peculiar type—to repre

sent the capitalist class; while on the other side
we have a series of vignettes of factory hands
too numerous to mention, boys and girls, men and
women, violent, eager, animated personalities,
each with a distinctive rôle in the evolution of
the story. Miss Mary Wilkins is not niggardly
in her portraiture. She pours before us all the rich
stores of her experience and her imagination.
Indeed, as has already been suggested, there is
too much wealth; we should have valued it more
if there had not been such a profusion of gold and
silver and copper in her medallions.

Only in the last place need the style be referred
to—full of a quiet beauty, never existing for its
own sake, strictly subordinate to the purposes of
the narrative. Here and there we have little gems
of description, carelessly strewn before us with
a regally profuse hand. "Ellen stroked her father's
thin grey hair with exactly the same tender touch
with which he had so often stroked her golden
locks. It was an inheritance of love, reverting to
its original source." Or take this: "After all,
friendship and good comradeship are a steadier
force than love, if not as overwhelming, and it
may be that tortoise of the emotions which out-
runs the hare." Or once more, dealing with the
effect of woman's beauty on man's devotion:
"'Jim don't act as if he thought so much of me,
an' I dunno as I wonder,' she told her sister. Fanny
looked at her critically. 'You mean you ain't
so good looking as you used to be,' said she. Eva

nodded. ' Well, if that is all men care for us,'
said Fanny. ' It ain't,' said Eva, ' only it's the
key to it. It's like losing the key and not bein'
able to get in the door in consequence.' " The
book is full of things like these, so full that they
are apt to be overlooked in the mass of material.
Nevertheless, from a purely artistic standpoint,
if we look solely at the best mode of expression
of which the authoress is capable, the verdict
must be that Miss Wilkins's supreme gift is the
pastel, not the historical canvas.

IV

When we come to her stories of the supernatural, it must be owned that they are strangely
disappointing. It is not, of course, given to every
one to interest, to absorb—to make us feel that
the unnatural is natural, to give us that delightful
shudder which is the essence of the true ghost-
story. But, so far as *The Wind in the Rose-Bush*
is concerned, such gifts clearly do not belong to
Miss Wilkins, and it seems a pity that she ever
consented to publish the book. She is so good a
narrator of the simple, the elemental, the prettily
pathetic; she draws with so sympathetic a pencil
the figures of a New England world which move
in response to easily discernible motives, and are
occupied with objects and interests of a wide and
familiar appeal, that, except from the point of
view of increasing her range and scope as a

novelist, it is difficult to see why she should have attempted to exercise her industry in new fields. Once, and once only, in the volume does Miss Wilkins attain her customary level, and then it is because she has hit upon a theme which is akin to her own instincts and predilections. In the last of her tales of the supernatural she tells the story of the ghost of a little child who had been abandoned and starved to death by an unfeeling mother—a pretty little pathetic figure of suffering with no language but the cry, " I cannot find my mother." It was a useful little ghost, assuredly, for if any one in the house which it haunted left wraps or cloaks about, or any strenuous house-wife desired to have plates washed and dried, the little child-ghost at once found an opportunity for helpful service. Moreover, its patience was fully rewarded in the sequel, for one of the two women who lived in the house, a childless widow, understood, by some process of maternal compre-hension, the forlorn little wastrel, and on her somewhat sudden death was seen taking the quite contented and happy child away with her in her arms. Here are just the elements of sentimental pathos which Miss Wilkins can manage, and the story is consequently quite an amiable piece of unartificial supernaturalism.

But of the others, what are we to say? They are almost grotesque in their suggestion of wholly trivial and unnecessary incidents; they have no power of translating us into another atmosphere;

they fail in the elementary condition of inspiring a pleasant terror. A woman discovers that a rose-bush can be violently agitated without any wind, and thereby is instructed that a niece of hers has been done to death. A brother has a dispute with another brother which ends fatally; he is therefore haunted by a shadow on the wall, and when in despair he does away with himself there are two shadows on the wall. A girl called Luella Miller, indolent, selfish, and fascinating, is apparently possessed of the diabolical power of slowly killing every one who is brought into contact with her. Perhaps she has the evil eye; perhaps she distils around her a subtle kind of poison. But whether she asserts her power consciously, or whether she is herself the victim of an unkind fate, we do not know, and we do not much care. To be told that at the last she is seen coming out of her house with all the ghosts of those whom she has done away with hanging on to her arms, and forming an uncanny retinue, might produce the requisite shiver if the writer had chosen to describe the scene with picturesque subtlety; but as the matter stands, Luella, whether agent of mischief or herself patiently expiating a curse, is wholly uninteresting. The case is the same with two other stories—" The South-West Chamber " and " The Vacant Lot." A fierce old aunt haunts the south-west chamber and plays stupid tricks, changing the counterpane on the bed and the hangings of the room, putting her own clothes back into the cupboard instead of the clothes of the visitor, and finally peering out of the looking-glass in which her niece only expected to find her own commonplace face. Or else, as in " The Vacant Lot," we have a troop of miserable-looking people in long gowns who occupy themselves with hanging up their own washing, or expressing mute indignation at an old signboard which had been made part of the panelling, and which in some dim way revived the memory of a long-forgotten crime. These are not the details which move and arrest the reader; they do not make him shudder; they only make him laugh.

There would be no point in criticising a book like this unless it suggested certain considerations on the proper use and management of the super-natural in fiction. Take the recognised literary successes in this department—the tales of Edgar Allan Poe, or some of the studies of Nathaniel Hawthorne, or those of Bulwer Lytton, or the weird suggestiveness of *Wuthering Heights*, or a book like *Uncle Silas*, by Le Fanu. The list could, of course, be prolonged indefinitely, for there are one or two tales of Mr. Henry James, of George Eliot, and of Mrs. Oliphant essentially worthy of notice in this reference. Under what conditions and by the exercise of what powers do writers like these manage to hold us enthralled? You may be as grotesque as you like, so long as you appeal to dominant feelings and passions in mankind. You may be quite arbitrary in the management of your plot, so long as you make the unnatural appear the necessary and the inevitable. You may deliberately take the moonlight as Hawthorne did—" moonlight in a familiar room falling white upon the carpet "—as the best medium for a romance-writer to get acquainted with his illusive guests. Or you may deal merely with the ordinary aspects of existence as Poe sometimes did, and yet make them instinct with some hidden and mysterious influences, bursting with a life alien from, and greater than their own. You may tell the reader from the very beginning that you are going to make his flesh creep, or you may take him by the hand in his ordinary habit as he lives, and, by a sudden whisk of the magician's rod, cause the solid things around him to disappear and the ordinary sunlight to change itself into some awful and glimmering gloom. But one indispensable condition throughout is that the writer of the ghost tale must be extremely careful and accurate in his detail in order to produce the illusion of verisimilitude. Not any kind of detail will suffice, however—Miss Wilkins uses a lot of detail—but it must be appropriate, suggestive, illuminative detail. It is of no use thinking that the change in a chintz from peacocks on a blue ground to red roses on a yellow ground, as in Miss Wilkins's " The South-West Chamber," causes us any thrill. We want rather that sudden shock which a detective officer might feel when some little point in the room he is exploring, or some bit of jewellery or adornment in the person suspected, suddenly confirms his anticipation or his theory—the kind of detail which Poe gives us in "The Murders of the Rue Morgue," "The Mystery of Marie Roget," "The Purloined Letter," and "The Gold Bug." Indeed, it is in the choice of the appropriate accessaries that a writer of supernatural romance shows his power.

But this is not all. A good ghost story must be really dramatic, and therefore involve a careful study and contrast of personalities. So far as can be seen, Miss Mary Wilkins is wholly devoid of the dramatic instinct; at all events, in her *Stories of the Supernatural* the personages are dull, characterless, lay figures. We want a real plot, which the *dramatis personæ* are to carry out for the most part unconsciously and unwillingly, a real struggle in their minds between what they would like to do and what they are forced to do, between free volition and tyrannical fate. It does not much matter whether we quite understand the intention of the author or not. Take, for instance, Hawthorne's stories, "The Wedding Knell," "Young Goodman Brown," "Roger Malvin's Burial." In these the meaning is certainly somewhat intricate and remote. But there must be a real study of character and situations, as, for instance, in Hawthorne's "Rappacini's Daughter"—a wonderful short story, which could easily have been expanded, had the author thought fit, into an elaborate romance. To live in other people's lives, to understand them better than they do themselves, to learn some secret about them of which they are for the most part unaware, to prove the inevitableness of fate, and the relative impotence of human activity—these things are the nerve and tissue of ghost stories, without which they may be, like Miss Wilkins's, pretty and graceful, or even like some of the stories of Mr. Hichens, curious and interesting, but cannot possess us with a sense of their reality, cannot grip and enchain us, like the best work of Hawthorne and Poe.

# THE CITY OF BATH

## By Arthur Waugh

When first I knew Bath—and it was the first town I ever saw with eyes hitherto accustomed only to country lanes—there was no railway to reach it from our own spur of the Mendips, and you drove across the coalfields of Radstock, by the long high road through White Post, up and down the rough places of Dunkerton Hill, with its lonely clump of dark trees upon the summit; and then, a few miles farther on, the hillside city broke upon your gaze, climbing up the side of what we used to be told was the crater of a dead volcano, tier above tier of crescents, and trees and spires. Is it only the tenderness of association, I wonder, that makes me believe that there is no city in England so thoroughly at one with itself in the spectacle it presents to the traveller's eye, so entirely and harmoniously a piece of definite architectural workmanship? Other tastes may acclaim other preferences, but for my part, my loyalty is unshaken.

Bath was indeed happy in the moment of its re-creation; the city, as we know it, grew up within a single century, at the will of a little company of master builders, fertile in taste and fancy. Everyone knows the old legend of Prince Bladud and the husks of the prodigal, of the swine that were healed in the mud baths, and of the Roman city, "Aquæ Solis"—waters of the sun—that grew up with this discovery of those mysterious powers. And the first known map of Bath, which issued from the Heralds' College in the second half of the sixteenth century, shows her then a fortified city of small dimensions, compact within her four gates, with the Avon to the south and east.

But this was not the city that we see to-day—far from it. Hard times settled upon the town during the Civil Wars, the baths themselves lost their repute, and for more than a hundred years scarcely a house was added to the map. And then, with the Restoration, there came changes. Charles II. and his Queen patronised the place; the Court began to talk about the excellence of the waters; and when, forty years later, Queen Anne paid a state visit to "the Bath," the turning-point in the fortunes of the town were reached. There was at once a great influx of fashionable life; the outlying villages of Weston and Twerton had to eke out the insufficient accommodation of the city itself; beds were a guinea a night, and the builders began to think that it was high time to be busy.

Then at last the city of Bath began to rise, climbing the terraced hill towards Lansdown, and using every shelving ridge to wonderful advantage.

Crescent rose above Crescent, and Place above Place; on the lower levels Queen Square and the Circus maintained a sort of courtly dignity; on the higher ground there was no room for wide display, and the precipitous street was flanked by rows of stately houses that took, with a natural sense of propriety, the shape of the hill they came to clothe. There was no haste or economy in the building; the houses were not only sound in fabric, but rich in decoration; the frontals finely wrought with pillars and garlands, the staircases wide and sunny, the ceilings beautifully adorned, the fireplaces tall and graceful; the whole city a place well suited to the fashionable life that was now to flood it with vivacity from Sydney Gardens to King's Mead, and from the Avon to Charlcombe Woods.

Is it sentimentality to feel that what is left of Bath to-day presents to the fond imagination little more than a grey and beautiful wraith of that city of wit and entertainment? The good Bathonian of the present day will indignantly deny the implication, protesting that the place is putting on its festal garb again, with dances in the springtime and a master of ceremonies all the year round—that the Queen of the West still knows how to reign among her apple orchards and her broken hills. It may be so; but to others the dances of to-day seem like a shadow pantomime, movement without colour, reflection without the heart of life. The streets of Bath, as one traverses them at midday at the beginning of the twentieth century, with their invalids in bath-chairs and their retired officers shuffling off to play bridge all the sunny afternoon in the club smoking-room, seem full of ghosts—the ghosts of Beau Nash and his merry men, who gaze upon the pageant with weary eyes, wondering if this indeed is the city of their merry prime. The old spirit has passed from Bath; the old days are done; what is left is a mere shadow of fantastic imagination.

But the city herself is there—a city of the eighteenth century, bland and beautiful, dreaming with her grey stone eyes of the glories of an unforgettable past. Many of her mansions have known what it is to have shop fronts driven into their carved façades; some of her chapels have changed into badminton courts and offices, and Beau Nash's private house is now a public theatre. But many more of the old buildings remain refreshingly unspoiled; the link extinguishers still survive amid the fine wrought-iron work; the interiors, with their lofty, garlanded ceilings and noble doors, are still unsacrificed to vandalism. Indoors and out the city keeps its old-world face for those who have time to linger and to look for it, and nowhere more than in the long Assembly Rooms, where the towering chandeliers glitter with suggestion of ancient lights, and the floor still shines from the polishing feet of the beaux and belles of a gayer generation.

What a world one can call up, standing in the

shadowy vestibule, and looking down the dim and empty hall; what life and spirit of

> The old Augustan days
> Of formal Courtesies and formal Phrase,
> The Ruffle's Flutter and the Flash of Steel.

Here Mrs. Malaprop grows garrulous over her cards; there Lydia Languish's eyelashes lift in answer to some quick retort; and surely that is Captain Absolute by the door, fresh and irresponsible as ever. Shadows of the past, flitting but imperishable! All memories of my native city are inextricably interwoven with your genial influence. You knew the city at her best, and, when we think of her then, we think of you as the brightest of her children. And, even though you are only creatures of the imagination, is not the world of the imagination the truest of all the worlds, after all?

And then the legends of the countryside! What county in the land can match them? It is here, perhaps, that one is apt to find the work of the historian a little distracting; it leaves you too few illusions. Old stories grow up around the country lanes, and are repeated from nurse to children; they become part of the heritage of the native; one likes them left unrifled by discovery. But when historical research comes along, it rules out the old map into squares, and sweeps away the landmarks of fancy. It serves, of course, the sacred cause of accuracy; but as one roams from Wells to Athelney, who wants to be too accurate?

Not I, at any rate; I love to fill my imagination, and the imaginations of my boys who will follow me on the old trails, with all the sweet, impossible lore of the countryside. For us Joseph of Arimathea shall return perpetually to the abbey by the marsh, with the Holy Grail and the sacred thorn in charge; for us the grave of Arthur shall remain a place of pious pilgrimage, so long as the feet will carry us and the eyes lift themselves up to the Mendip Hills. "Hic jacet sepultus inclytus rex Arturus in insula Avalonia," and here we will still reverence his legend without questioning too carefully whether Queen's Camel were really Camelot.

And there are other stories, too, probably entirely built of fancy. When I was a little boy, I was told how all the valley round Shapwick was once the summer sea, and how the waters came up right to the foot of Glastonbury Abbey. And the story further ran that here it was that the dusky barge came up, "Dark as a funeral scarf from stem to stern," and carried Arthur, with his three Queens, into the confines of the spiritual city. And, further, I was assured that Sir Bedivere climbed the face of Glastonbury Tor itself to see the last of the spectral vessel, "straining his eyes beneath an arch of hand," until the vision was lost in the light. The story is, of course, all apocryphal; doubtless it is demonstrably false. Yet for one believer no later knowledge can sweep away the childish impression; and I shall never

see Glastonbury Tor lifting above the sunlight and
shadow without a thought of Bedivere and Arthur;
and of the eventual passage awaiting every soul—
" From the great deep to the great deep he goes."

And is not this typical of so much of the early
associations of childhood, the secret of those " first
affections, those shadowy recollections," which,
however deeply the plough of anxious years may
drive the furrow through our hearts,

> Are yet the fountain-light of all our day,
> Are yet a master-light of all our seeing;
> Uphold us, cherish, and have power to make
> Our noisy years seem moments in the being
> Of the eternal Silence.

These, after all, are the real things of life; not
the counting-house, the printing-press, the pen
and ink and paper of a grinding Duty; but the
imaginings with which we set out upon the day's
journey; the light that never was except in
dreamland; the voices that never spoke but to
the ear of the soul. And is not this the reason
that the old homeward way always finds every
one of us a child again? What is it but this
longing to revive the heart of childhood that leads
our feet so often to the old, familiar hills?

> Hame, hame, hame, O hame fain would I be—
> O hame, hame, hame, to my ain countree!

It is not only, of course, that the trees are
greener, and the winding roads whiter among the
fields of home. The Roman colonist, when he left
his father's house, used to take with him some of

the glowing coals from the hearth, and set them down alight on the new hearthstone in the new home. It was a beautiful idea, and all of us would choose to do the same; but it does not conclude the whole matter. Some of the home-spirit may travel with us across the sea, but the better part of it remains inseparable from its birth-place. It was here that we were young; here that we first hoped; here that we first loved. And when youth, and hope, and love are all at an end, it is here that we would choose to rest, returning, like the hunted stag, to the spot where we were roused, and losing all remembrance in the land which memory has always kept unspoiled and unspotted from the world.

# SHAW AND SWIFT

## By H. W. Massingham

Shaw's part in modern literature has been that of
the critical rather than the creative artist ; and as
this is the account he renders of himself in one of
the most interesting, of his dramatic prefaces,[1]
it is unnecessary to labour the point. He ought,
he tells us, to have set out to be from the first
the "iconographer" of the religion of his time.
He preferred to describe its institutions by way
of a series of comedies of manners, wrought in
the ironical manner. In this he was wrong. He
should have set out for Damascus earlier, for
his consciousness had all along told him that
civilisation needed a religion, "as a matter of
life and death." But somehow the call did not
come. So instead of an "iconographer" he became
an iconoclast, content to play his part in the
destruction of Bibliolatry and other fetishes. Then
he grew dissatisfied. Mechanistic evolution proved
as inadequate as Paley's Grand First Watchmaker.
How had the universe really come to be what it is,
and Adam had breathed into him the divine spark
that made him a living soul? And how had his

[1] *Back to Methuselah : A Metabiological Pentateuch.* By
Bernard Shaw. (Constable.)

descendants, misled as they were by the legendary
form of their religion into taking it for literal fact
instead of for spiritual truth, contrived, with all
their superstitions, to follow the light that always
shone within and above and beyond them? Well,
the revealing and redemptive word came at last.
It was " Creative Evolution." Man was a spirit,
capable of assisting the divine purpose, but, like
Shaw, postponing the effort. Then he decided
to will to live longer, and Shaw immortalises
the effort in his *Metabiological Pentateuch*, otherwise commended under the more popular title of
" Back to Methuselah."

Now it is clear that for a child of this retroces-
sive age, or even a little of the age to come, the
attempt to exhibit and forecast the spiritual
ascent of man is very difficult. If in such an hour
the eye of faith can still perceive the advance, the
sensitive literary mind may well fail to discover
what point of fresh and inspiriting departure
remains for the discouraged souls and polluted
fancies of the survivors of the Great War. It is
singular that a great writer, one of the greatest,
pursuing his theme of the baseness of mankind,
hit upon the same expedient as Shaw has devised to figure forth the hope of a divine issue
to its adventure on earth. Swift conceived the
idea of the lengthening of the average term of
human life and invented the Struldbrugs. Shaw
has devised the Ancients. We must leave the
readers of the *Voyage to Laputa* and of *As Far*

*as Thought can Reach* to make their choice between the picture of the self-regarding man reduced to helpless dependence and that of intellectual virtue relieved of the temptation to possessive or even altruistic affection. That they are comparative studies in decay, neither Swift confronted with Shaw, nor Shaw confronted with Swift, would deny. Swift, indeed, knew nothing of evolution, creative or mechanical. But he had one thing in common with Shaw, in addition to wit and a wonderful art in writing. He hated human passion, having indeed a fearfully sharpened sense of the part it played in his own life and in the world of war and politics and sensual intrigue into which he was born. And it seemed to him that the more you prolonged the term of man, the worse, or at least the more pitiful, he got. Shaw, as truly benevolent as Swift, and with much the same intellectual view of contemporary life, but more good-natured, has had the happy notion of moralising the Struldbrugs. So he eviscerates them. His human beings of the perfectible period, ovarian in origin, are allowed four quarrel-some years of love and devotion to art. The centuries that remain to be lived through are given to contemplation. Sex remains, but so attenuated as to be hardly worth noticing. The fighting instinct—the Cain-man—has gone alto-gether. Shaw calls this Elysium 30,000 years hence. Really it is the Island of Laputa over again. The scientists are in power, having, it

appears, overcome their present inclination to
disintegrate the atom and make a Shakespearean
clearance of the last Act of Man's drama on the
earth. But they are as absurd as ever. They have
seen to it that Man's soul is preserved, but that it
kills his body, while a speculative (and presumably
spectacled) being awaits in chill resignation a fresh
creative or destructive impulse arising in the
inventive soul of Lilith.

It will be asked what space is left in this
shadow-world of Shaw's for the religious idea with
which he identifies his later dramatic work, and
of which " Back to Methuselah " is, he hints, to
be the final illustration. Is it either religious or
scientific? A certain number of supermen will
to live for three hundred years. In spite of
Weismann, this " acquired modification " is im-
parted, until it reaches out to a natural immortality, bar accidents. But what of the mass of
mankind? Shaw rather contemptuously consigns
them to the class of " short-livers," who
appear to be mainly Britons, with Imperial
headquarters in Baghdad. Presumably they die
out, or, as in the case of the elderly English
gentleman in Part IV., are assassinated by the
supermen. But with the loss of the Socialist
conception of the rise of humanity *en masse*,
all the warmth dies out of the idea of social
progress. It becomes ascetic and Manichæan.
In his expository preface Shaw rightly distin-
guishes Goethe, the Olympian, from the pessimist

Shakespeare and the realist Ibsen, the critical and irreligious dramatists of intellectual Europe. For Goethe, like Swedenborg, had seized the Pauline conception of ascent from Adam, the first Man, to the second, who is the Lord from Heaven. And so he reserved for his Faust an active and fruitful old age, passing, in the final content of accomplishment, into the rapture of redeemed and purified love. But there are no raptures for Shaw. Man's Cosmic Experience is for him the tearing of one illusion after another from the skin of a carnal and hypocritical creature. "We were well enough in the garden," he makes the ghost of the toiling, unimaginative Adam cry at the close of his sombre retrospect of what is rather a thin, qualitative selection than a generous process of creative evolution. Yes, indeed; if the end of all his toil was to eliminate not only the egoistic perversity of man, but effort and affection, and to leave him mooning round an animal-less sphere, from which pain and strife have disappeared, while wisdom swallows up good, leaving itself equally devoid of object and content. Shaw makes Lilith, the mystical mother of birth, describe this arrival at the gates of death, figured as if they were the only heaven of which man was capable:

They have taken the agony from birth; and their life does not fail them even in the hour of their destruction. Their breasts are without milk; their bowels are gone; the very shapes of them are only ornaments for their children to admire and caress without understanding.

What, then, has been accomplished? Man has cured himself of his vileness, and Cain, the first murderer, lies buried with his innumerable progeny of the violent and the unredeemed. Of Life itself there cannot well be an end; the vast landscape of creation will always fade into a populous " beyond." But the reign of the spirit in the human heart is merely the signal for the slowing down of its tumultuous heat, and God reappears as the pale Avatar of annihilation.

It seems to me to be quite natural for Hamlet-Shaw to end thus, though it hardly justifies him in cutting formally loose (as he has so often done) from the pessimism of Shakespeare. Shaw, even when in nominal pursuit of State Socialism, was always, like Swift, a pessimistic rationalist, bravely dropping seeds of liberty and truth into the spirit of man. His pilgrimage has shown him that Man does not live long enough to attain to either, and so he gives him three hundred years in which (with the help of science) to try again. But even in the act of creative evolution he discovers that there is nothing much to evolve, only a great deal to purge and cast away. What was to be done in the way of spiritual progress with a creature of such violent and endemic irrationality as Man? For sixty years Shaw had seen and observed it in the attractive guise of God's Englishman. What could he make of such a being? He was a wit and an Irishman. What beauty could he see in Imperialism? An acutely sensitive critic of art, he was too much of a Puritan to become its devotee. It belonged to the childhood and the enthusiasm of the past. Shaw's powers of style and self-expression gave him a hold on these two worlds of British idealism and British Philistinism; but something incurably fastidious in his nature has always forbidden him to conceive a truly religious affection for the human being. For a killing, vivisecting, flesh-eating, coarsely love-making, woodenly selfish, and yet absurdly complacent animal like that, the best that Shaw could predict was a deliverance from the body of its death. That was as far as his thought would reach. His artist wings have never been quite strong enough to carry him into the mystic region where both the Christian and the humanist poet saw God as the centre of radiant energy, eternally renewed. Sick of materialism in life and thought, he has turned, he says, to metaphysics. In reality, he ends as a Christian heretic, a Manichee of the twentieth century.

The style and artistry of this long series of fabulist plays, with their provoking and energetic preface, are unequal. The opening scene in the Garden of Eden, and of the Serpent's incitement to the adventure that is to end in nothing, is a masterpiece, easily and beautifully playable, and it is a pity that Shaw could not carry on his concise, dramatic start to the end of his journey. The middle is a halt for political comedy by the way. The close catches up the lost philosophical idea of the enterprise, and restores it to dignity and spiritual consequence. Here the child-lover frolics butterfly-like on the scene, before the shades of ancient wisdom close on her and on the disillusioned artists who follow her brief morn. Here the He and She Ancients appear and retire to their groves and mountains, morosely contemplating a world that is already dead. Here the ghosts of the past—of the Adam who toiled and willed, of the Eve who was curious, of the Serpent who tempted, and introduced laughter and death to the world—revisit the glimpses of a moon-like earth, where the weak live for ever, while Lilith, the deputy-creator, preaches the funeral sermon of humanity. It is an impressive, a poetic conclusion. But it is not the attainment of God. It is the fall of the leaves of the **Tree** of **Life.**

# OF COMFORT

## By Henry W. Nevinson

It is a queer word, that "Comfort." It appears to have come down in the world. We suppose from the look of it that once it meant something that added strength or courage or fortitude, and the original meaning is seen in the old Statute of Treasons, which defines treason as "comforting the king's enemies." Fairly early it came to imply a mental consolation or solace, as we see in the words, "Comfort ye, comfort ye, my people," and "Rachel mourning for her children, and would not be comforted." Then there is the proverb about Job's Comforters, and we have known "cold comfort," which meant much the same as the consolation given to Job. That high or spiritual meaning still persists. One hears an old woman sometimes saying that her son, or even her husband, is a "great comfort" to her, and the poet writes of "comfort scorned of devils." But in its commonest use the word has degenerated. When we speak of comfort, we generally think of an easy, warm, and restful state of body or bodily surroundings. We mean "creature comforts," or "home comforts," implying pleasant furniture and plenty to eat. When we say that a family is " in comfortable circumstances," we mean that life is pretty easy for it. A " comfortable person " is easy-going and inclined to be stout. A " comforter " has so little reference to Job that it has become a woollen scarf.

There is something peculiarly English about the word. Though a French hotel may advertise *Conforts du premier ordre*, all foreigners recognise the English claim. A few years ago there was a fairly well-to-do Athenian who was far from content with the illustrious glories of his city. In vain the Acropolis revealed to him by day and night the noblest monuments of architecture. In vain Lycabettus rose in pellucid air, and the bay of Salamis glowed like amethyst, and purple Hymettus hummed with all its bees. No history, art, or nature could soothe his restless soul. For he had been in England, and " Nothing," he cried, " nothing on earth makes life worth living but solid English comfort! " England's solid comfort had given him a glimpse of an earthly Paradise, and in his own City of the Violet Crown he mourned uncomforted. One remembers how the Yorkshire servant who accompanied Kinglake upon his journey through Servia and Bulgaria, then almost as desolate under Turkish rule as now under Christian atrocities, " rode doggedly on in his pantry jacket, looking out for ' gentlemen's seats.' " It was for the English comfort of gentlemen's seats that the poor fellow was looking, unable to imagine a country so god-forsaken as to be without it. Similarly, I have known a wealthy travelling Englishman regretfully informing his Turkish host that in England we always have marmalade for breakfast. And two English ladies, compassionately eager to give relief to distressed Albania, wrote to inquire whether the railways were comfortable there and the lavatories clean; and the only possible answer was that in Albania there are neither railways nor lavatories.

That solid English comfort, how pleasingly fond memory paints it! The large and airy bedroom with dark blinds, the early tea brought in by the white-aproned maid, the hot shaving-water and cleaned boots, the large washing-basins, the white porcelain bath, the copious breakfast with coffee or tea and choice of varied flesh, fowl, and eggs upon the sideboard, the smoking-room with deep armchairs and a mingled savour of cigars and peaty tweeds, the healthy and appetising exercise with horse or fishing-rod or gun, the copious lunch, which perhaps appeared by the butler's magic in the woods, the bland hours of afternoon, just pleasantly stirred by the clink of tea-cups, the leisurely converse upon animals and birds and fishes, hardly interrupted by the copious dinner, and continued till whisky-and-soda with sandwiches announced the approach of welcome bedtime. Or (not to leave out the intellectual stimulus so essential for complete well-being) the perusal of the *Times* and the sporting papers in the

morning, the large library with card-tables, the
rows of well-bound books with readable titles, the
occasional references to politics and the ruin of
the country, and perhaps a walk to church with
the ladies on Sunday, to encourage the poor and
listen in somnolent peace to the voices of vicar and
choir-boys among the ancient arches. What other
land has ever incubated a life of such comfort
as that? The disgruntled satirist may sniff at
"Heartbreak House" and "Horseback Hall."
Never mind! No country but ours has evolved
such solidity of comfort, and the further the
comfort withdraws into the abysm of time the
more we dwell upon it with poignant regret.
Rhoda Broughton was no more gourmand than
the rest of us, yet with what pathos, in old age,
in her posthumous novel, she laments the passing
of once familiar joys:

The unbidden tears rise to my eyes [she writes], as
I look back upon the fat breasts of those Aylesbury
ducks across the desert of the late lean years. Then
they were commonplaces of daily life, and did not
even provoke an admiring ejaculation, any more
than did their handmaids, the exquisite marrowfat
peas in their tender juvenility.

It is true there are various standards of comfort,
differing chiefly according to income. Some find
comfort in a Kensington flat or maisonnette; some
in the ignobly decent monotony of a suburban
street. Some are content when they have attained
to a best parlour, where books lie upon the table

like spokes in a wheel and the india-rubber plant in the window sheds an almost religious shade. We remember what pride filled old Clayhanger's heart when at last he won for himself a dwelling whose front door opened into a passage instead of a room. The " working people " (the average men and women of every country) cling to their " bits of things " as evidences of respectability and realities of comfort, and grudgingly part with them to the pawnshop when times are hard. It is made a bitter reproach to them if they purchase fur coats and jewellery or even clothe the children well when times are good; yet, within their narrow limits, they are only imitating the ideal of necessary comfort held by their " betters," who certainly are not working people. Comfort is largely a matter of comparison. All who were out upon any fighting front during the war know how comfortable, how luxurious even, the ordinary things of life appeared to them on their return—the real bread-and-butter, the table-cloth, the plentiful soap-and-water, the bed with sheets. Even after a journey to foreign parts, Catullus knew that feeling of unaccustomed but familiar peace:

Oh, what is more blessed than release from anxieties? [he wrote] when the soul lays aside its burden, and wearied with exertions abroad we reach our own hearth and settle snugly down in the bed we have so pined for.

It is largely a matter of comparison, but the trouble is that when they have become accustomed

to one degree of comfort, people are very unwilling
to descend to another. We can imagine that some
would miss the tea brought up to the bedside,
some the marmalade for breakfast, some the
Aylesbury ducklings, some the deep armchairs,
some the porcelain bath, some the aproned maid,
some the *Times*, some the indiarubber plant. The
German nobleman thinks it hard to remove from
his ancestral Schloss into a desirable villa residence.
The Russian Grand Duke is dissatisfied with a
workman's food and clothing, even though the
Soviet workman's standard of life may have
advanced. The learned Professor does not enjoy
returning to the attic which seemed quite jolly
when he was a student. Fear of losing comfort
to which people are accustomed or have risen has
an incalculable influence even upon our votes.
It acts as a drag on politics, national and inter-
national. " Behold the bulwarks of the Constitu-
tion!" cries the comfortable man, restoring his
confidence by a walk through suburban villas. Skin
for skin, yea, all that other people have, will a
man give for his comfort. He will also block the
way to all that other people ought to have. For
comfort is the life-breath of reaction, and that is
why England has long been the most Conservative
of countries, being the Daniel Lambert of nations,
as George Meredith once called her.

But our Daniel Lambert is shrinking now, and
the skin begins to hang loose about his opulent
limbs. One need not consider only the rumours

of strikes and revolutions and Bolshevism to know the change that is indubitably upon us. Read the news about the sales of great country houses and estates. Heartbreak House collapses; Horseback Hall fades like a vision. Profiteers, glutted like ghouls with noble blood, may flourish for the moment, but they too will shrink and fade. Already one sees the belted Earl wondering whether it is really necessary to his salvation to have a castle in the north, a mansion in the south, a house in Grosvenor Square, and a villa on the Mediterranean, involving so much perplexity in which of them to live. Already great town mansions are splitting into flats, fissiparous as jelly-fish. Already our country gentry are taking paying guests and teaching them what English comfort was. The shrinkage proceeds downwards right through all the comfortable classes — down through the "people of independent means" to the hard-working professional men and women. "Beautiful it is," cried Carlyle two generations ago, "to see the idol of old Mammon cracking in all directions!" The idol was patched up for a time, but now it cracks still more visibly, and we do not deny it is a beautiful sight. But a lot of comfort goes with it, and the loss does not look so beautiful.

What, then, shall we do? With the pound note valued at something over ten shillings, we have become a poor country instead of being a rich, and we must adapt ourselves to the change. At what we should properly call the worst, each plane of the comfortable classes must come down a degree or two in comfort, the castle living at the standard of the mansion, and the mansion at the standard of the villa, and so on down the scale of wealth and shrinkage. At what, we suppose, we ought to call the best, there will be a general rise in the degrees of comfort for the average men and women who work daily for wages, and a proportional fall for the comfortable classes, the severity of the fall varying directly with the distance. That Earl's fall, for instance, right down to the level of comfort "in widest commonalty spread," will be like Mulciber's when he fell sheer over the crystal battlements of heaven and landed on barren Lemnos Isle. But to the humble journalist the jolt or bump will hardly be perceptible. In any case, we have encouraging examples. How pleasant it is to read of those American Indians who burnt all their furniture and other possessions once a year and started fresh and clean! And let us recall the list of comforts that Thoreau took with him to the woods— a list that sounds almost superfluously long:

A bed, a table, a desk, three chairs, a looking-glass three inches in diameter, a pair of tongs and andirons, a kettle, a skillet, a frying-pan, a dipper, a wash-bowl, two knives and forks, one cup, one spoon, a jug for oil, a jug for molasses, and a japanned lamp.

He added a book or two, but we think an Earl would find it quite possible to curtail that list in other ways as well. The first thing for us to do, as the portentous change creeps upon us, is to restore the original meaning of that word " comfort." It has degenerated until it implies a certain amount of softness, torpor, and imbecility. We must restore it to its birthright as something contributing to strength, courage, or fortitude. Then, with the poet of America, we can cry:

> Not for delectations sweet,
> Not the cushion and the slipper, not the peaceful and the
> studious,
> Not the riches safe and palling, not for us the tame
> enjoyment!
> Do the feasters gluttonous feast?
> Do the corpulent sleepers sleep?  have they locked and
> bolted the doors?
> Still be ours the diet hard, and the blanket on the ground!

But one hopes that by that time those questions will be needless, for there will then be no gluttonous feasters, no corpulent sleepers, no locks and bolts, no doors, except to keep out the cold.

# THE PILGRIM FATHERS

## By John Masefield

The Brownist emigration, known to Americans as the "Sailing of the Pilgrim Fathers," was a little part of a great movement towards independence of judgment in spiritual affairs. The great movement began in the latter half of the sixteenth century in many parts of England. The little part of it which concerns us began in the early years of the seventeenth century in the country about the borders of the three counties of Nottingham, Lincoln and York. The Separatists were members of the lower and middle classes, who accepted the ruling of the Church of England in articles of faith, but refused her judgment in points of discipline. They held (in opposition to the Church) that the priesthood is not a distinct order, but a office temporarily conferred by the vote of the congregation.

Their attitude and action have been thus described by one of their number: "*They entered into covenant to walk with God and one with another, in the enjoyment of the Ordinances of God, according to the Primitive Patern in the Word of God. But finding by experience they could not peaceably*

*enjoy their own liberty in their Native Country,*
*without offence to others that were differently minded,*
*they took up thoughts of removing."*

One party of them, under Pastor John Smyth,
" removed " from Gainsborough, in Lincolnshire,
to Amsterdam in the year 1606. Another party
organised in that year in the district of Scrooby,
in Nottinghamshire, about ten miles west from
Gainsborough, began to make itself obnoxious
to the country authorities. This second party
contained two prominent men, William Brewster,
the chief layman, and John Robinson, one of
the two ministers.

The members of the party were accustomed to
meet together " to worship God in their own
manner." Church discipline, which forbade their
meetings, imposed a persecution upon them.
Religious persecution that endeavours to drive
a flock along a path is successful, as a rule, only
with the sheep. It makes the goats unruly. The
persecution failed to bend the brethren, but it
gave them enough annoyance to make them wish
to leave the country. The leaders among them
planned an exodus to Holland. In the autumn of
1607 a large party tried to escape to Holland from
the port of Boston, in Lincolnshire. At that time
it was not lawful for a person to leave the country
without licence. A large party could not hope to
get away without the connivance of a ship's
captain. The ship's captain to whom this escaping
party appealed accepted the bribe, then, fearing

the consequences of his action, or hoping to obtain a reward, betrayed his passengers to the authorities. The members of the party were sentenced to a month in gaol;· their goods were confiscated. Later in the year, another party was stopped while trying to escape from Great Grimsby. Many women and children were taken and imprisoned.

The prisoners in country gaols were then supported out of the rates. The keeping of large numbers of people in prison, in idleness, proved to be a great burden upon the rates of the towns where they were gaoled. The authorities who felt the burden soon became anxious to get rid of their prisoners. They released them and connived at their leaving the country. By August 1608 the whole party was safely in Amsterdam.

During the next few months, after some contention with the party from Gainsborough, a hundred of the Scrooby party obtained leave to go to Leyden, where they settled down to the manufacture of woollen goods. They were joined from time to time by other Separatists from England. In a few years their communion numbered some three hundred souls, among whom were Edward Winslow, John Carver, and Miles Standish.

In the year 1617 these exiles began to realise that Holland, though a seasonable refuge, could not be their abiding place. The children were growing up. The parents did not wish to send them to Dutch schools, because the Dutch children were of bad behaviour. The parents feared that the children, if sent to school in Holland, would receive evil communications and lose something of their nationality. No one is so proud of his nationality as the exile. The fear that the colony might become a part of the Dutch population caused the leaders to think of travelling elsewhere. Guiana, the first place suggested, was rejected as unsuitable, because it was supposed to contain gold. Gold, or the prospect of finding gold, would be a temptation, if not a curse, to weak members of the community. There was also the prospect of danger from the Spaniards. Virginia, the next place suggested, was considered unsafe. The English were there. It was doubtful whether the English would allow in their midst a large community the members of which held unauthorised religious opinions. No other place offered such advantages as Virginia. The settlers there were Englishmen and Protestants. It was decided that members of the community should go to London to ask leave of the Virginia Company. In September 1617 two of the Separatists (John Carver and Robert Cushman) laid before the Virginia Company in London a declaration in seven articles. This declaration was designed to show that the Separatists would not be rebellious nor dangerous colonists. It stated that they assented to the doctrines of the Church of England and acknowledged the King's authority. The Virginia Company, accepting the declaration, was inclined to welcome the party as colonists; but a fear, suggested by the bishops, that they intended for Virginia " to make a free popular state there " caused delay. The patent was not granted till the 9th–19th of June, 1619.

When the patent had been obtained more delay was caused by the difficulty of obtaining money for the equipment of the expedition. The London merchants saw little prospect of rich returns. They were slow to invest in an undertaking so hazardous. It was one thing to subscribe money " for the glory of Christ and the advancement of the beaver trade," another to equip a large party of religious enthusiasts for an experimental settling in a savage country. John Robinson, wearying of the delays, tried to persuade the Dutch to encourage the party to settle in the New Netherlands. His request led to nothing. Early in 1620, Thomas Weston, a London merchant, suggested that the settlement should be made in Northern Virginia. About seventy other merchants offered to subscribe. The business began to go forward. A Common Stock was formed. Ten pound shares in this Stock could be taken either by money or by goods. John Carver went to Southampton to engage a ship. Robert Cushman, acting for the brethren, drew up an agreement with the merchant adventurers, or, as we should call them, the speculators. He agreed that all the labour of the colonists should be for the common benefit, and that, after seven years, the results of the labours (houses, tilled land and goods) should be divided equally between the planters and the adventurers.

Although some seventy merchants subscribed money, the Common Stock was not big enough to send all the brethren to America. The majority had to stay in Holland. Those who chose, or were chosen, to go, left Leyden for Delft Haven, where they went aboard the ship *Speedwell*, of sixty tons, which had been bought and equipped in Holland. On or about the 10th–20th of July, 1620, the *Speedwell* sailed for Southampton.

At Southampton, the emigrants found waiting for them the ship *Mayflower*, of 180 tons. She was a London ship, chartered for the occasion. In her were other emigrants, some of them labourers, some of them Separatists eager to leave England. With them was the chief adventurer, Mr. Thomas Weston, who had come to ask the leaders of the party to sign the contract approved by Cushman. As the leaders did not like the terms of the contract they refused to sign it. There was an angry dispute. In the end Mr. Weston went back to London, with the contract not signed.

It had been agreed that he was to advance them another sum of money before the ships set sail. As the contract was not signed, the pilgrims had to manage without this money. Without it, they found it difficult to pay the charges of the ships and crews. They were forced to sell sixty pounds' worth of provisions to obtain money for the

discharge of these claims. In those days, and, indeed, until within the memory of men now living,
passengers across the Atlantic lived upon supplies
of food laid in and prepared by themselves. The
Western passage was seldom made in less than
two months. The pilgrims could not hope for any
fresh supply of food before the next year's harvest
in the New World. A considerable lessening of
their stock of provisions might well lead to the
ruin of the settlement.

About the 5th–15th of August the two ships put
to sea in company, carrying in all about 120
emigrants. After eight days, the captain of the
*Speedwell* complained that his ship had sprung a
leak. The expedition put back into Dartmouth
to refit. On setting sail again, the ships beat a
hundred leagues to the west of the Land's End,
when they were forced, by stress of weather, to
put back into Plymouth. The captain of the
*Speedwell* declared that his ship was too much
battered to keep the seas. Though the man was
lying in order to escape from the fulfilment of his
charter, his word was taken. The *Speedwell* was
abandoned, the pilgrims in her were bidden to
come aboard the *Mayflower* to take the places of
some who could endure no more. About twenty
of the pilgrims left the expedition at Plymouth.
They were discouraged by the hardship and sea-
sickness, two doctors which never fail to teach the
unfit that though many are called to the life of
pioneers, very few are chosen. Among those who

left the expedition at Plymouth was Robert Cushman.

On Wednesday, the 6th–16th September, the expedition left Plymouth for a third attempt. In the existing records little is said about the voyage; but it must have been a strange and terrible adventure to most of the party. The ship was very small, and crowded with people. Counting the crew, she must have held nearly a hundred and fitfy people, in a space too narrow for the comfort of half that number. The passengers were stowed in the between-decks, a sort of low, narrow room, under the spar deck, lit in fine weather by the openings of hatchways and gun-ports, and in bad weather, when these were closed, by lanterns. They lived, ate, slept, and were sea-sick in that narrow space. A woman bore a child, a man died there. They were packed so tightly, among all their belongings and stores, that they could have had no privacy. The ventilation was bad even in fine weather. In bad weather, when the hatches were battened down, there was none. In bad weather the pilgrims lived in a fog, through which they could see the water on the deck wash-ing from side to side, as the ship rolled, carrying their pans and clothes with it. They could only lie, and groan, and pray, in stink and misery, while the water from ill-caulked seams dripped on them from above. In one of the storms during the passage, the *Mayflower* broke her mainbeam. Luckily one of her passengers had a jackscrew, by means of which the damage was made good. But the accident added the very present fear of death to the other miseries of the passage.

The *Mayflower* made the land on the 9th–19th November, after a passage in which the chief events were the storm, birth and death above mentioned. On coming towards the shore the landfall was seen to be the strange curving crook of Cape Cod, in Massachusetts. The pilgrims' patent was for a settlement in Virginia, far to windward in the south. There was no settlement of white people at Cape Cod. As they had made the land so far to the north the pilgrims thought that their best plan would be to beat down to the Hudson River and look for a place near the Dutch settlement in what is now New York. The crew of the ship refused to do this. Winter was coming on. They were not disposed to beat down a dangerous coast, to a doubtful welcome, in the teeth of the November gales. They told the pilgrims that they must go ashore where they could. Men were sent ashore to examine the land. On the 11th November the pilgrims met together " to covenant and combine themselves together into a civil body politic." The whole party numbered 102, of which 73 were male and 29 female. More than half of the number had come from Leyden. The covenant was signed by forty-one men, seven of whom were labourers. John Carver was selected the first governor of the community.

During the next few weeks, parties of the pilgrims

searched for a good site for the settlement. On the 22nd of December the site was found in the grounds adjoining what is now Plymouth Harbour. The *Mayflower* was brought into the harbour, and on Monday, 25th December, the first house was begun. By the middle of January most of the pilgrims were ashore.

It is said that their first winter in the New World was mild. It was certainly very terrible to them. Want of fresh food, the harshness of the change of climate, the exposure and labour in the building of the town, and the intense cold of even a mild New England winter, were more than they could endure. Nearly half of them were dead within six months. Among the dead was the governor, John Carver, who died shortly after his re-election to office. His place was taken by William Bradford. In the early spring of 1621, an Indian called Samoset came to the pilgrims. He told them that the place where they had settled was called Patuxet, and that the Indians had deserted those parts owing to an outbreak of the plague. The *Mayflower*, sailing back to England in April, carried with her a tale of great mortality and the prospect of possible pestilence when the hot weather came.

The summer proved fine, and the harvest good. In November, by which time less than fifty of the original settlers remained alive, Robert Cushman arrived among them, in the ship *Fortune,* with thirty-five recruits (ten of them women). He also brought a patent (granted by the President and Council of New England), allowing to each settler a hundred acres of land and the power to make laws and govern. In December 1621, in a letter sent home in the ship *Fortune*, the settlement was first called New Plymouth.

The after history of the settlement may be indicated briefly. It is a story of the slow but noble triumph of all that is finest in the English temper. By honest industry and by that justice which, until the last two generations, usually marked and ennobled our dealings with native tribes, the settlement prospered. The pilgrims honestly paid the Indians for the lands acquired from them. In 1623 they were able to stop an Indian war, which had been provoked by some intemperate colonists, sent out by Thomas Weston to a place twenty miles to the north of New Plymouth.

In 1624, the London merchants sent out one John Lyford to be clergyman to the community. He was sent home for trying to set up the ritual of the Church of England. Another clergyman, who was sent to them four years later, went mad.

In 1626, many of the London adventurers were bought out. They surrendered their shares for the sum of eighteen hundred pounds, payable in nine yearly instalments. Eight leading planters and four principal merchants in London undertook to make the first six payments in return for the monopoly of the foreign trade. In the reorganisation of the company the most prosperous men of the community were made stockholders. They were allotted one share for each member of their families. Each head of a family was granted an extra acre of land, and a title to his house. The cattle, being still few in number, were allotted among groups of families. Few laws were made, though the men sometimes met in General Court to discuss public business.

In 1630, when the second charter arrived, the colony numbered three hundred souls. After that time, its growth was slow, steady, and not very eventful, till the disastrous Indian war of 1676. In 1691 it was merged in the bigger " civil body politic " of Boston.

Emigration nowadays is seldom an act of religious protest, still more seldom an endeavour to found a more perfect human state. Man emigrates now to obtain greater personal opportunity, or in tacit confession of incompetence. When he emigrates in protest, it is in æsthetic protest. The migration is to some place of natural beauty, in which the creation of works of art may proceed under conditions pleasing to their creators.

A generation fond of pleasure, disinclined towards serious thought, and shrinking from hardship, even if it may be swiftly reached, will find it difficult to imagine the temper, courage and manliness of the emigrants who made the first Christian settlement of New England. For a man to give up all things and fare forth into savagery, in order to escape from the responsibilities of life, in order, that is, to serve the devil, " whose feet are bound by civilisation," is common. Giving up all things in order to serve God is a sternness for which prosperity has unfitted us.

Some regard the settling of New Plymouth as the sowing of the seed from which the crop of Modern America has grown. The vulgarity of others has changed the wood of the *Mayflower* into a forest of family trees. For all the *Mayflower's* sailing there is, perhaps, little existing in modern England or America " according to the Primitive Patern in the Word of God." It would be healthful could either country see herself through the eyes of those pioneers, or see the pioneers as they were. The pilgrims leave no impression of personality on the mind. They were not " remarkable." Not one of them had compelling personal genius, or marked talent for the work in hand. They were plain men of moderate abilities, who, giving up all things, went to live in the wilds, at unknown cost to themselves, in order to preserve to their children a life in the soul.

# THOMAS HUXLEY

## By Sir Oliver Lodge

It has been fortunate for the intellectual interest of
life that the peace-loving Darwin and the self-effacing
Wallace should have had a coadjutor more vividly touched
with earthly fire, like the mortal charger who, champing
more fiercely in the battle's fray, kept pace with the two
undying steeds of Achilles. But we must remember that
Professor Huxley's trenchant polemic has cast a kind of
glory about the mere fact of man's ignorance which cannot
possibly be kept up for long. Battles there will always be;
but never again, perhaps, such a plunging through half-
armed foemen, such an ἀριστεία of the Agnostic such a
record of individual triumphant feats], as we associate
with that brilliant name.

F. W. H. Myers (Essay on *Charles Darwin and Agnosticism*).

Yes, battles there will always be, and Huxley
was a splendid fighter, but the ostensible cause
for which he fought—insistence on our present
ignorance and on the folly of pretending to
know what in truth we do not—is not a cause
of satisfying fullness.

Ignorance, it is right to confess, but it is never
a thing to glory in. Only in an age in which
rash assertion and mistaken tradition dominated
thought too strongly was the flag of the Agnostic
a conquering and triumphant emblem.

The battle has already shifted to other grounds;
and before the end of his life Huxley realised that

a great part of his warfare on the negative side was accomplished, and that it remained to restrain his camp-followers from prowling too savagely among the dead and wounded.

The essential and permanent aspect of his teaching, like the teaching of all men of science, lies on the positive side; and here effort is still necessary, for, though a great deal has been accomplished, the scientific training and interest of the average educated man is still lamentably deficient. Nor are the attempts to remedy the deficiency, as carried out in schools and colleges, always of the wisest and happiest kind. Nevertheless an effort is being made; and when things have settled down into their due proportion, future generations will recognise how much they owe to the preachings and teachings, the lay sermons and lectures, of Huxley.

The supremacy of truth, the reality of things, the cultivation of the senses, the need for realistic education and understanding of the physical universe in the midst of which man is set, the folly of yielding to mere glamour, and the sin of sophisticating what we can perceive of truth by hope of reward or dread of consequence—all this he strenuously fought for; and surely we may say that on the whole he won. No recognised branch of natural knowledge is now excluded from contemplation by reasonable men, nor is stringent inquiry cursed or dreaded, even by those to whose general purview it appeared at one time to be alien. The universe is recognised as one; and loyal allegiance must be accorded to every proven fact.

The battle is now transferred from this general contention to a more special one:—What range of facts can we admit into the category of positive knowledge? How much wider can we make the area of rational contemplation? Shall the human race be for ever limited to the domain of ether and atoms alone—as W. K. Clifford imagined—or are there other existences, just as real, just as important, just as well worthy of study, just as deserving of scrutiny by scientific methods?

It was no attack on Religion that Huxley led, it was an attack on the *præjudicia* of religion— the bland assumptions which did duty for reasoning, the self-interested arguments which concentrated attention on the past, attempted to despise the present, and held out illusory hopes for the future.

Study the universe before you, the living universe, with its traditions and history incorporated in it; cease to limit yourselves to the fancies and speculations of more ignorant times: that was Huxley's message.

A piece of chalk, he said, rightly interpreted, will tell you more about the physical history of the world than myriads of books. Try and learn the language of the chalk—"it is easier than Latin," so he said; and whoso knows the true history of a bit of chalk in a carpenter's pocket "is likely, if he will think his knowledge out to its ultimate results, to have a truer, and therefore a better, conception of this wonderful universe, and of man's relation to it, than the most learned student who is deep-read in the records of humanity and ignorant of those of nature."

This is language appropriate to intellectual warfare. It is part of his battle-cry, it is an emphatic statement of one side of the truth, it is not the whole truth. Its comparative side is its weak side: it is not really necessary to decry other forms of learning in order to exalt one—and Huxley showed later that he did not think so; it was only because one side was being neglected, and the other was in possession of the field, that he stood up manfully for the outcast, and dragged it into a prominent position.

The comparative side of his utterance was pugnacious, and therefore temporary, but the positive side is eternally true. Every bit of chalk *is* related to all the rest of the universe; and he who would know all about it—the life of the creatures whose remains compose it, its past, present, and future in all its phases—must have a grasp of the universe beyond the present scope of man. Tennyson said the same thing, more poetically, in his "Flower in the crannied wall."

But granting all this, what then? Because we are not to jump to conclusions too rapidly, because we must make our bearings and foundations sure, because our hopes and predictions must be well founded—is there to be no future, no hope for the

human race? Is the end of all human struggle
and effort to coincide with the probable end of the
solar system—a dark, dead, lifeless lump careering
through the depths of space? That were to reason
too curiously to reason so.

Darwin could not contemplate such an ending
—his instinct rebelled against it. In a notable
passage he expresses the placid disbelief of an
open-eyed investigator in such a conclusion—
an investigator to whom the avenues of knowledge
were in this direction closed, and who therefore
would make no assertion one way or the other,
but who instinctively felt that there must be
some other answer. This he says:

"Believing as I do that man in the distant
future will be a far more perfect creature than he
now is, it is an intolerable thought that he and
all other sentient beings are doomed to complete
annihilation after such long-continued slow
progress."

And Tennyson, in his poem "Despair," has
dramatically and impersonally voiced a violent
development of the same feeling:

Why should we bear with an hour of torture, a moment of
    pain,
If every man die for ever, if all his griefs are in vain,
And the homeless planet at length will be wheel'd thro'
    the silence of space,
Motherless evermore of an ever-vanishing race,
When the worm shall have writhed its last, and its last
    brother-worm will have fled
From the dead fossil skull that is left in the rocks of
    an earth that is dead?

And again in " Vastness ":

> What is it all, if we all of us end but in being our own
>     corpse-coffins at last,
> Swallow'd in Vastness, lost in Silence, drown'd in the deeps
>     of a meaningless Past?

But in the fighting age such instincts and feelings and longings had rigorously to be suppressed. They were too perilously near the old bulwarks of superstition, which were to be broken down. Hence the side of assured positive knowledge was to be kept in the van—there was indeed plenty to do—and a more comprehensive understanding of the puzzles of existence might wait until some positive knowledge began to appear, throwing the light of day upon them also.

While things remain in the dark they must be ignored. This is the basis of the Agnostic position. Flashes of speculation inevitably broke around it, and the hope was not lacking that "out of the molecular forces in a mutton chop Hamlet or Faust could be deduced by the physics of the future." But this enthusiastic and more than half-playful utterance of Tyndall (*Life and Letters of Huxley*, i. 231) is showing itself baseless—as baseless and as alien to the truly Agnostic position as any of the superstitions that were then being attacked. Nevertheless, it is an interesting sign of the enthusiasm kindled by the physical discoveries of the nineteenth century—interesting and quite intelligible, and in its way legitimate—for readers of the present day should learn where to emphasise, and where to discount, the utterances of the teachers of an enthusiastic and a fighting age.

Here, for instance, is the conclusion that Huxley draws from his piece of chalk, which, like lime exposed to the oxy-hydrogen flame, had become luminous under his scrutiny, so that "its clear rays, penetrating the abyss of the remote past, have brought within our ken some stages of the evolution of the earth. And in the shifting 'without haste but without rest' of the land and sea, as in the endless variation of the forms assumed by living beings, we have observed nothing but the natural product of the forces originally possessed by the substance of the universe."

Yes, that is a narrowly logical position. Keep rigidly to scrutiny of the material universe, and nothing beyond matter and force shall you discover. The conclusions that you draw will be entirely appropriate to the data. Things belonging to Cæsar will be rendered unto Cæsar. Of things not so belonging it need not yet be the time to discourse.

It would be a great mistake to assume that in all his contentions Huxley was right: we can imagine his sarcasm at the notion of infallibility in connection with his utterances. In a few cases he went, in my judgment, seriously wrong; and, led astray by controversial successes, he occasionally inflicted undeserved blows upon causes which had much of good in them and which might have flourished with his help—upon such a cause as the early efforts at social work of the Salvation Army, for instance. And, by his concentrated insistence on the material side of things, he sometimes led his hearers to imagine that it was the only side that mattered, or even the only one that existed. Nevertheless it was not really against Religion that Huxley was wielding his battle-axe: it was against the Fetishism, the Polytheism, the Theism or Atheism and many other isms, with the relative merits and demerits of which, as he said, he had nothing to do: " But this it is needful for my purpose to say, that if the religion of the present differs from that of the past, it is because the theology of the present has become more scientific than that of the past; because it has not only renounced idols of wood and idols of stone, but begins to see the necessity of breaking in pieces the idols built up of books and traditions and fine-spun ecclesiastical cobwebs : and of cherishing the noblest and most human of man's emotions, by worship ' for the most part of the silent sort ' at the altar of the Unknown and Unknowable."

Here again we encounter a glorification of the Unknown God, which, as was implied before, cannot for ever, nor for long, be an object of rational worship. The intellectual business of the human race, and of scientific investigators, is to attack the Unknown and to make it, so far as possible, gradually known. Never completely known, nor at all adequately known, but never unknowable. Infinite things cannot be grasped by finite comprehension—in that sense unknowable, yes, but in no other. The universe itself is unknowable, in the sense of being infinite; but the human aspect of it is open to our examination and comprehension—with that we have kinship and instinctive affinities—and it would only confuse the issue, and muddy the stream of scientific exploration, if we were to start on our quest with the idea that anything whatever was in any real and practical sense "unknowable."

To be able to ask a question is the first step towards getting an answer. There must be myriads of things in the universe about which it has never occurred to a human being to formulate any sort of idea. Those truly are outside our present ken; but anything of which we can discourse and think—that is on the way, by patience and perseverance and rigorous care and truthfulness, to become known.

The discourse of Huxley's on "A Liberal Education," which he gave to working men, is worthy of close attention, especially among the higher artizans who are determining to get for themselves, if so they can, and for their children still more, the advantages of some approach to a liberal education.

It is not the whole truth which he there expresses, it is one aspect of the truth—an aspect

SIR OLIVER LODGE

that then needed emphasis more than it does now. It is the view of an individual man, but of a profoundly wise and cultivated man, who would never wish us to limit our grasp of truth to an understanding of his own utterance, but would ask us to listen and progress further. What he is anxious about is that we shall not lag behind.

The metaphor of a game of chess is employed by Huxley as a parable of life:

"The chess-board is the world, the pieces are the phenomena of the universe, the rules of the game are what we call the laws of nature. The player on the other side is hidden from us. We know that his play is always fair, just, and patient. . . . My metaphor will remind some of you of the famous picture in which Retzch has depicted Satan playing at chess with man for his soul. Substitute for the mocking fiend in that picture a calm, strong angel, who is playing 'for love' as we say, and would rather lose than win, and I should accept it as an image of human life."

A little farther on comes a passage, often quoted, about the strict discipline of physical nature:

"Ignorance is visited as sharply as wilful disobedience—incapacity meets with the same punishment as crime. Nature's discipline is not even a word and a blow, and the blow first; but the blow without the word. It is left to you to find out why your ears are boxed."

And presently comes that magnificent sentence

about control of the passions, which I quote in order to draw to it special attention.

" That man, I think, has had a liberal education who has been so trained in youth that his body is the ready servant of his will, and does with ease and pleasure all the work that, as a mechanism, it is capable of; whose intellect is a clear, cold, logic engine, with all its parts of equal strength, and in smooth working order; ready, like a steam engine, to be turned to any kind of work, and spin the gossamers as well as forge the anchors of the mind; whose mind is stored with a knowledge of the great and fundamental truths of nature and of the laws of her operations; one who, no stunted ascetic, is full of life and fire, but whose passions are trained to come to heel by a vigorous will, the servant of a tender conscience; who has learned to love all beauty, whether of nature or of art, to hate all vileness, and to respect others as himself.

" Such an one and no other, I conceive, has had a liberal education."

The petty Agnostics who, invoking the shade of Huxley, look out of their little holes and corners, peer through a foggy atmosphere, and deny the stars, have no support from their great precursor. He would counsel them to see life steadily and see it whole, and to remember that the greatest men are not those who blink difficulties and claim that they have done more than they have, but those who modestly admit every difficulty, and where they are ignorant conspicuously avow it.

To those, for instance, who imagine that Darwin discovered the whole truth about the origin of species, by his undoubtedly just emphasis on struggle for existence and survival of the fittest —since these influences tend to clinch and make permanent the variations which otherwise arise —to those who imagine that we understand fully the origin of those variations, without which natural selection would have nothing to work upon, let us quote the following from Huxley's controversial reply to foreign critics of Darwinism. It is an extract from an utterance of Darwin himself:

"Our ignorance of the laws of variation is profound. Not in one case out of a hundred can we pretend to assign any reason why this or that part varies more or less from the same part in the parents."

Lastly, in these days when women have come so much to the front, and are showing signs of occasionally even over-complete emancipation, it is well to remember that only half a century ago the cause of their rational and higher education had to be fought. Huxley's article on "Emancipation—Black and White," an outcome of the American Civil War, is a plea for giving a fair field and no favour.

"Emancipate girls," he says. "Let them, if they so please, become merchants, barristers, politicians. . . .

"Woman will be found to be fearfully weighted in the race of life. . . .

"The duty of man is to see that not a grain is piled upon that load beyond what nature imposes; that injustice is not added to inequality."

So, then, we come to the more technically scientific lectures, the biological teaching of which he was a master. He discusses, among other things, the probable origin of the human race—whether it spread from one centre or from many—and evidently inclines to the view that human evolution took place at only one point of the earth's surface, and was distributed over it by migration. But on this he does not dogmatise: the alternative views have difficulties of their own. The nascent stages of humanity must have been delicate and dangerous in the extreme, and it seems unlikely that the process of evolving man would be often repeated, at different places, on a planet. But then it is difficult to contemplate any form of uncivilised migration which from a centre in, say, Asia could reach and populate the American continent down to Patagonia.

"The whole tendency of modern science is to thrust the origination of things farther and farther into the background; and the chief philosophical objection to Adam [is], not his oneness, but the hypothesis of his special creation."

Most of this part of the present book consists of a course of lectures on the skull and its development. The various stages of the human skull, and of the animal skull, are dealt with, and their points of similarity and difference emphasised.

To any one who doubts the physical ancestry of man, as part of the animal world, these chapters will bear the meaning which they are intended to convey.

But if any one at this time of day thinks that physical ancestry is the last word, and exhausts the meaning of human genesis and of what may be meant by "Adam,"—any one who thinks that Spirit and Genius and Inspiration offer no field for investigation, furnish no clue to interpretation, and are foreign to any rational study of the human race, the possibilities of which are exhausted by an exemplary scrutiny of dry bones—such an one would wrest the teachings of the learned among mankind and apply them to his own stultification.

It is not by denying and restricting that we progress, it is by examining the ground and advancing, without haste, without rest, till we reach fresh woods and pastures new. Admitting those things which are behind, and reaching forward to those things that are before—that is the attitude of the genuine explorer of nature, for all time.

The truth of one set of things is quite compatible with the truth of many another set of things. Only let the truth in every age be established, and let no corner of the universe—physical, mental, moral, spiritual—be closed to patient and reverent investigation.

To those few unfaithful pastors who dare not admit the plain teachings of modern science, and to those many pathetic half-educated strivers after knowledge who think it their duty to deny everything else, I say:

Oh, race of men, be worthy of thy heroes. Look not back on bones and lowly ancestors alone as exhausting the truth of the universe; learn the lessons these things can teach, and bethink yourself also of the triumphs of mind over matter; realise the dominion of music and poetry and science and art; and remember, when tempted to take a low and depressed view of humanity, that during our own days we have had living with us, on this small island, a Darwin, a Tennyson, and a Huxley.

# THE ROSE

## By Logan Pearsall Smith

THE old lady had always been proud of the great rose-tree in her garden, and was fond of telling how it had grown from a cutting she had brought years before from Italy, when she was first married. She and her husband had been travelling back in their carriage from Rome (it was before the time of railways), and on a bad piece of road south of Siena they had broken down, and had been forced to pass the night in a little house by the roadside. The accommodation was wretched of course; she had spent a sleepless night, and rising early had stood, wrapped up, at her window, with the cool air blowing on her face, to watch the dawn. She could still, after all these years, remember the blue mountains with the bright moon above them, and how a far-off town on one of the peaks had gradually grown whiter and whiter, till the moon faded, the mountains were touched with the pink of the rising sun, and suddenly the town was lit as by an illumination, one window after another catching and reflecting the sun's beams, till at last the whole little city twinkled and sparkled up in the sky like a nest of stars.

# THE ROSE

That morning, finding they would have to wait while their carriage was being repaired, they had driven in a local conveyance up to the city on the mountain, where they had been told they would find better quarters; and there they had stayed two or three days. It was one of the miniature Italian cities with a high church, a pretentious piazza, a few narrow streets and little palaces, perched, all compact and complete, on the top of a mountain, within an enclosure of walls hardly larger than an English kitchen garden. But it was full of life and noise, echoing all day and all night with the sounds of feet and voices.

The Café of the simple inn where they stayed was the meeting-place of the notabilities of the little city; the *Sindaco*, the *avvocato*, the doctor, and a few others; and among them they noticed a beautiful, slim, talkative old man, with bright black eyes and snow-white hair—tall and straight and still with the figure of a youth, although the waiter told them with pride that the *Conte* was *molto vecchio*—would in fact be eighty in the following year. He was the last of his family, the waiter added—they had once been great and rich people —but he had no descendants; in fact the waiter mentioned with complacency, as if it were a story on which the locality prided itself, that the *Conte* had been unfortunate in love, and had never married.

The old gentleman, however, seemed cheerful enough; and it was plain that he took an interest in the strangers, and wished to make their acquaintance. This was soon effected by the friendly waiter; and after a little talk the old man invited them to visit his villa and garden which were just outside the walls of the town. So the next afternoon, when the sun began to descend, and they saw in glimpses through doorways and windows, blue shadows beginning to spread over the brown mountains, they went to pay their visit. It was not much of a place, a small, modernised, stucco villa, with a hot pebbly garden, and in it a stone basin with torpid gold fish, and a statue of Diana and her hounds against the wall. But what gave a glory to it was a gigantic rose-tree which clambered over the house, almost smothering the windows, and filling the air with the perfume of its sweetness. Yes, it was a fine rose, the *Conte* said proudly when they praised it, and he would tell the Signora about it. And as they sat there, drinking the wine he offered them, he alluded with the cheerful indifference of old age to his love affair, as though he took for granted that they had heard of it already.

" The lady lived across the valley there beyond that hill. I was a young man then, for it was many years ago. I used to ride over to see her; it was a long way, but I rode fast, for young men, as no doubt the Signora knows, are impatient. But the lady was not kind, she would keep me waiting, oh, for hours; and one day when I had waited very long I grew very angry, and as I walked up and down in the garden where she had told me she would see me, I broke one of her roses, broke a branch from it; and when I saw what I had done, I hid it inside my coat—so—; and when I came home I planted it, and the Signora sees how it has grown. If the Signora admires it, I must give her a cutting to plant also in her garden; I am told the English have beautiful gardens that are green, and not burnt with the sun like ours."

The next day, when their mended carriage had come up to fetch them, and they were just starting to drive away from the inn, the *Conte's* old servant appeared with the rose-cutting neatly wrapped up, and the compliments and wishes for a *buon viaggio* from her master. The town collected to see them depart, and the children ran after their carriage through the gate of the little city. They heard a rush of feet behind them for a few moments, but soon they were far down toward the valley; the little town with all its noise and life was high above them on its mountain peak.

She had planted the rose at home, where it had grown and flourished in a wonderful manner; and every June the great mass of leaves and shoots still broke out into a passionate splendour of scent and crimson colour, as if in its root and fibres there still burnt the anger and thwarted desire of that Italian lover. Of course the old *Conte* must have died many years ago; she had forgotten his name, and had even forgotten the name of the mountain city that she had stayed in, after first seeing it twinkling at dawn in the sky, like a nest of stars.

# THE HILL-TARN

## By Fiona Macleod

Isolated, in one of the wildest and loneliest mountain-regions of the Highlands of Ross, I know a hill-tarn so rarely visited that one might almost say the shadow of man does not fall across its brown water from year's end to year's end. It lies on the summit of a vast barren hill, its cradle being the hollow of a crater. Seven mountains encircle Maoldhu from north, south, east, and west. One of these is split like a hayfork, and that is why it is called in Gaelic the Prong of Fionn. Another, whose furrowed brows are dark with the immemorial rheum of the Atlantic, is called the Organ of Oisin, because at a height of about two thousand feet it shows on its haggard front a black colonnade of basalt, where all the winds of the west make a wild and desolate music. I have heard its lamentation falling across the hill-solitudes and down through the mountain-glens with a sound as of a myriad confused sobs and cries, a sound that is now a forlorn ecstasy and now the voice of the abyss and of immeasurable desolation. Another, that on the east, is an unscalable cone, from whose crest, when sunrise flames the serrated crags into a crown of burning bronze, the golden eagle sways like a slow-rising and slow-falling meteor. All day, save for a brief hour at noon, shadow dwells about its knees, and never lifts from the dark grassy lochan at its feet. It is called Maol Athair-Uaibreach, the Hill of the Haughty Father: I know not why. "The Haughty Father" is a Gaelic analogue for the Prince of Darkness—son of Saturn, as he is called in an old poem: "God's Elder Brother," as he is named in a legend that I have met or heard of once only— a legend that He was God of this world before " Mac Greinne " (lit.: Son of the Sun) triumphed over him, and drove him out of the East and out of the South, leaving him only in the West and in the North two ancient forgotten cities of the moon, that in the West below the thunder of grey seas and that in the North under the last shaken auroras of the Pole.

It is not easy to reach this tarn of Maoldhu even when the hillways are known. The mountain-flanks have so vast a sweep, with such wide tracts of barren declivity, where the loose stones and boulders seem to hang in the air like a grey suspended fruit though the first tempest will set them rolling in avalanche. There are so many hidden ravines, and sudden precipices that lean beneath tangled brows like smooth appalling faces; on the eastern slopes the mountain-sheep cannot climb more than half-way; on the south and west the wailing curlews are in continual flight above wide unfrontiered reaches of peat-bog and quaking morass; so many crags lead abruptly to long shelving ledges shelterless and slippery as ice, and twice an abyss of a thousand feet falls sheer from loose rock covered by treacherous heather for a yard or more beyond the last gnarled, twisted roots.

But, when it is once reached, is there any solitude in the world more solitary than here? The tarn, or lochan rather—for if it is not wide enough to be called a loch it is larger than the ordinary tarn one is familiar with on high moorlands and among the hills—has no outlook save to the lonely reach of sky just above it. A serrated crest of herbless and lifeless precipice circles it. On the lower slopes a rough grass grows, and here and there a little bog-myrtle may be seen. At one end a small dishevelled array of reed disputes the water-edge, in thin, straggling, disconsolate lines. There is nothing else. Sometimes the ptarmigan will whirr across it, though they do not love crossing water. Sometimes the shadow of an eagle's wing darkens the already obscure depths. But the mountain-sheep never reach this height, and even the red deer do not come here to drink these still, brown waters: "One sees no antlers where the heather ceases," as the shepherds say. The clouds rise above the crests of the west and pass beyond the crests of the east: snow, the steel-blue sleet, the grey rains, sweep past overhead. In summer, a vast cumulus will sometimes for hours overlean the barren crater and fill the tarn with a snowy wonderland and soft abysses of rose and violet: sometimes a deep, cloudless azure will transmute it to a still flame of unruffled, shadowless blue. At night, when it is not a pit of darkness to which the upper darkness is twilight, it will hold many stars. For three hours Arcturus will pulsate in it like a white flame. Other planets will rise, and other stars. Their silver feet tread the depths in silence. Sometimes the moon thrusts long yellow lances down into its brooding heart, or will lie on its breast like the curled horn of the honeysuckle, or, in autumn, like a floating shell filled with fires of phosphorescence. Sunset never burns there, though sometimes the flush of the afterglow descends as on soft impalpable wings from the zenith. At dawn, in midsummer, long scarlet lines will drift from its midmost to the south and west, like blood-stained shafts and battle-spears of a defeated aerial host.

Few sounds are heard by that mountain-tarn. The travelling cloud lets fall no echo of its fierce frost-crashing shards. Dawn and noon and dusk are quiet-footed as mist. The stars march in silence. The springing Northern Lights dance in swift fantastic flame, but are voiceless as the leaping shadows in a wood. Only those other wayfarers of the mountain-summit, tempest, thunder, the streaming wind, the snow coming with muffled rush out of the north, wild rains and whirling sleet, the sharp crackling tread of the hosts of frost:

only these break the silence; or, at times, the cries of "the eldest children of the hill," as the mountain-Gael calls the eagle, the hill-fox, and the ptarmigan—the only creatures that have their home above the reach of the heather and in the grey stony wildernesses where only the speckled moss and the lichen thrive.

When I was last at this desolate and remote tarn I realised the truth of that hill-saying. After the farthest oaks on Sliabh Gorm, as the ridge to the south-west is called and up which alone is a practicable if rough and often broken way, came scattered groups and then isolated trees of birch and mountain-ash. Thereafter for a long way the heather climbed. Then it gave way more and more to bracken. In turn the bracken broke like the last faint surf against huge boulders and waste stony places. The grouse called far below. The last deer were browsing along their extreme pastures, some five hundred to eight hundred feet below the precipitous bastions of Maoldhu. Higher than they I saw a circling hawk and three ravens flying slowly against the wind. Then came the unpeopled wilderness, or so it seemed till I heard the wail of a solitary curlew (that spirit of the waste, for whom no boggy moors lie too low and desolate, for whom no mountain-ranges are too high and wild and solitary), and once, twice, and again in harsh response but faint against the wind, the barking of a hill-fox and its mate. All life had ceased, I thought, after that, save an eagle which in a tireless monotony swung round and round the vast summit of Maoldhu. But suddenly, perhaps a hundred feet above me, six or seven ptarmigan rose with a whirr, made a long sailing sweep, and settled (slidingly and gradually as flounders in shallow waters among grey pebbles and obscuring sand-furrows) among the lichened boulders and loose disarray of speckled granite and dark and grey basalt and trap—an ideal cover, for even a keen following gaze could not discern the living from the inanimate.

Truly the eagle, the hill-fox, and the ptarmigan are " the eldest children of the hill." The stag may climb thus high too at times, for outlook, or for the intoxication of desolation and of illimitable vastness; sometimes the hawks soar over the wilderness; even the mountain-hares sometimes reach and race desperately across these high arid wastes. But these all come as men in forlorn and lonely lands climb the grey uninhabitable mountains beyond them, seeking to know that which they cannot see beneath, seeking often for they know not what. They are not dwellers there. The stag, that mountain-lover, cannot inhabit waste rock; the red grouse would perish where the ptarmigan thrives and is content.

How little has been written about these birds of the mountain-brow. What poetry is in their name, for those who know the hills. They dwell higher than the highest June-flight of the tireless swift, higher than the last reaches of the sunrise-

leaping larks. Cities might crumble away in pale
clouds of dust, floods might whelm every low-
land, great fires might devour the forests and the
red insatiable myriad of flame lap up the last
high frontiers of bracken and climbing heather,
and the ptarmigan would know nothing of it,
would not care. Their grey home would be in-
violate. No tempest can drive them forth. Even
the dense snows of January do not starve them
out. Do they not mock them by then taking the
whiteness of the snow for their own? They have
nothing to fear save the coming of a black frost
so prolonged and deathly that even the sunfire
in the eagle's blood grows chill, and the great
pinions dare no more face the icy polar breath.
"They'll be the last things alive when the world
is cold," said an old gillie to me, speaking of these
storm-swept lichen-fed children of the upper-wild.

The same old gillie once saw a strange sight at
my mountain-tarn. He had when a youth climbed
Maoldhu to its summit in mid-winter, because of
a challenge that he could not do what no other
had ever done at that season. He started before
dawn, but did not reach the lochan till a red fire
of sunset flared along the crests. The tarn was
frozen deep, and for all the pale light that dwelled
upon it was black as basalt, for a noon-tempest
had swept its surface clear of snow. At first he
thought small motionless icebergs lay in it, but
wondered at their symmetrical circle. He des-
cended as far as he dared, and saw that seven

wild swans were frozen on the tarn's face. They had alit there to rest, no doubt: but a fierce cold had numbed them, and an intense frost of death had suddenly transfixed each as they swam slowly circlewise as is their wont. They may have been there for days, perhaps for weeks. A month later the gillie repeated his arduous and dangerous feat. They were still there, motionless, ready for flight as it seemed.

How often in thought have I seen that coronal of white swans above the dark face of that far, solitary tarn: in how many dreams I have listened to the rustle of unloosening wings, and seen seven white phantoms rise cloud-like, and like clouds at night drift swiftly into the dark; and heard, as mournful bells through the solitudes of sleep, the *honk-honk* of the wild swans traversing the obscure forgotten ways to the secret country beyond sleep and dreams and silence.

# WINTER STARS

## By Fiona Macleod

### I

To know in a new and acute way the spell of the nocturnal skies, it is not necessary to go into the everlasting wonder and fascination of darkness with an astronomer, or with one whose knowledge of the stars can be expressed with scholarly exactitude. For the student it is needful to know, for example, that the Hyades are Alpha, Delta, Eta, etc., of Taurus, and lie ten degrees south-east of the Pleiades. But as one sits before the fireglow, with one's book in hand to suggest or one's memory to remind, it is in another way as delightful and as fascinating to repeat again to oneself how Tennyson in *Ulysses* speaks of this stellar cluster as

> Thro' scudding drifts the rainy Hyades
> Vext the dim sea . . .

or how Christopher Marlowe wrote of them:

> As when the seaman sees the Hyades
>   Gather an army of Cimmerian clouds,
> Auster and Aquilon with winged steeds . . .

to recall how Spenser alludes to them as "the Moist Daughters," or how our Anglo-Saxon

ancestors called them " the Boar-Throng." One
must know that Alpha of Boötes is the astronomical
signature of the greater Arcturus, but how much
it adds to the charm of this star's interest for us
to learn that among its popular names are the
Herdsman, the Bear-Watcher, the Driver of the
Wain, and to know why these now familiar names
were given and by whom. One may grasp the
significance of the acquired knowledge that this
vast constellation of Boötes stretches from the
constellation of Draco to that of Virgo, and the
numeration of its degrees in declination and
ascension, and (if one may thus choose between
the 85 and the 140 of astronomers) that it contains
a hundred stars visible to the naked eye. But,
for some of us at least, there is something as
memorable, something as revealing, in a line such
as that of the Persian poet Hafiz, as paraphrased
by Emerson,

Poises Arcturus aloft morning and evening his spear—

or that superb utterance of Carlyle in *Sartor
Resartus*,

What thinks Boötes of them, as he leads his Hunting
Dogs over the zenith in their leash of sidereal fire ?

Not, I may add in parenthesis, that the seekers
after astronomical knowledge should depend on
the poets and romancers for even an untechnical
accuracy. Literature, alas, is full of misstate-
ments concerning the moon and stars. Few poets
are accurate as Milton is magnificently accurate,

his rare slips lying within the reach of a knowledge achieved since his day: or as Tennyson is accurate. Carlyle himself, quoted above in so beautiful a passage, has made more than one strange mistake for (as he once aspired to be) a student astronomer: not only, as in one instance, making the Great Bear for ever revolve round Boötes, but, in a famous passage in his *French Revolution*, speaking of Orion and the Pleiades glittering serenely over revolutionary Paris on the night of 9th August, 1792, whereas, as some fact-loving astronomer soon pointed out, Orion did not on that occasion rise till daybreak. It has been said of the Moon, in fiction, that her crescents and risings and wanings are to most poets and novelists apparently an inexplicable mystery, an unattainable knowledge. Even a writer who was also a seaman and navigator, Captain Marryat, writes in one of his novels of a waning crescent moon seen in the early evening. The great Shakespeare himself wrote of the Pole Star as immutable, as the one unpassing, the one fixt and undeviating star :

> . . . constant as the Northern Star,
> Of whose true fixed and lasting quality
> There is no fellow in the firmament.

This was, of course, ignorance of what has since been ascertained, and not uninstructedness or mere hearsay. Possibly, too, he had in mind rather that apparent unchanging aloofness from the drowning sea-horizon to which Homer alludes in the line beautifully translated " Arctos, sole

star that never bathes in the ocean wave " . . .
of which, no doubt, our great poet had read in
the quaint delightful words of Chaucer (rendering
Boetius)—" Ne the sterre y-cleped ' the Bere,'
that enclyneth his ravisshinge courses abouten the
soverein heighte of the worlde, ne the same sterre
Ursa nis never-mo wasshen in the depe westrene
see, no coveitith nat to deyen his flaumbe in the
see of the occian, al-thogh he see other sterres
y-plounged in the see."

That constellation " y-cleped the Bere," how
profoundly it has impressed the imagination of
all peoples. In every age, in every country, our
kindred on lonely lands, on lonely seas, from
caverns and camp-fires and great towers, have
watched it "incline its ravishing courses " about
the Mountain of the North, "coveting not "
to drown its white fires in the polar seas. Here,
however, it is strange to note the universality of the
Ursine image with the Greeks and Romans and
the nations of the South, and the universality
with the Teutonic peoples of designations such as
the Wain and the Plough. It was not till the
Age of Learning set in among the Northern peoples
that the classic term came into common use.
Thus in a tenth-century Anglo-Saxon manual
of astronomy the writer, in adopting the Greek
Arctos (still used occasionally instead of the
Bear), adds "which untaught men call Carles-
wæn," that is Charles's Wain, the Waggon. A
puzzling problem is why a designation which

primarily arose from an association of the early
Greeks concerning Arkas, their imaginary racial
ancestor, with Kallisto his mother, who had been
changed into a great bear in the heavens, should
also suggest itself to other peoples, to races so
remote in all ways as the North American Indians.
Yet before the white man had visited the tribes
of North America, the red men called the constellation by names signifying a bear. The historian Bancroft has proved that alike among the
Algonquins of the Atlantic and of the Mississippi,
among the Eastern Narragansett nations and
among the nations of the Illinois, the Bear was
the accepted token.

Boötes, the Great Bear, the Little Dipper or
Ursa Minor, these great constellations, with their
splendid beacons Arcturus, the Triones or the
Seven Hounds of the North, and the Pole Star—

By them, on the deep,
The Achaians gathered where to sail their ships—

and in like fashion all the races of man since Time
was have " gathered " the confusing ways of night
on all lonely seas and in all lonely lands.

But best of all, to know this spell of the nocturnal
skies, one should be in the company of fisher-folk
or old seamen or shepherds, perchance unlettered
but wise in traditional lore and leal to the wisdom
of their fathers. How much more I value what
I have heard from some shepherd on the wide
dark moors, or from some isleman in a fishing-
coble or drifting wherry, on moonless nights

filled with a skyey " phosphorescence " as radiant
as that a-dance and a-gleam in the long seethe
of the wake of a ship, than what I have found
concerning scientific star-names in books of
astronomy. Nothing that I have since learned
of " the Pointers " has impressed me so much
as what I learned as a child of " the Hounds of
Angus," nor, in later and fuller knowledge of
Polaris, has the child's first knowledge of the
mystery and wonder of " the Star of Wisdom,"
as pointed out and tale-told by an old Hebridean
fisherman, or of " the House of Dreams," as sung
to me in a forgotten ballad by a Gaelic woman
of Argyll, been surpassed.

It was they — herdsmen and mariners, the
wayfarer, the nomad, the desert-wanderer—who,
of old, gave these names to which the nations
have grown used. It was with the nomad that
astronomy began. The Chaldæan shepherd, the
Phœnician mariner, studied the stars and named
them and the great constellations which group
themselves from horizon to horizon in the nocturnal
skies. They perceived strange symmetries, symbolic images, grotesque resemblances. The same
instinct made the Arab of the Desert call the
Pleiades the Herd of Camels, made the Akkadian
call them the Wild Doves, made the Celtic hunter
call them the Pack of Hounds, made the Teuton
peasant call them the Hen and Chickens, made
the Australian savage call them (in conjunction
with the Bear) Young Girls playing to Young

Men dancing: the same instinct, this, as made
the ancient poet of the Zend-Avesta call them
the Seven Beneficent Spirits, or made the modern
poet of *Locksley Hall* liken them to a swarm of
fireflies, or made the Gaelic poet of to-day image
them as the Herring-Net. In a word, the instinct
of poetry: which is as deep as hunger and thirst,
as deep as love, as deep as fear, as deep as the
desire of life. The instinct of the imagination to
clothe the mysterious and the inexplicable in the
raiment of the familiar or of recognisable and
intimate symbol.

How infinitely it adds to the beauty of a star-
name such as Aldebaran, or Alcyone, or Polaris,
to know that to the swarthy nomads of the desert
it imaged itself as one following in a skyey desert,
a camel-driver tracking lost camels, a hound
following a quarry, a warrior following a foe,
a holy pilgrim tracking the difficult ways of God,
so that no name seemed to them so apt as *Al
Dabarān*, the Follower: to know that to the
pastoral Akkadians or the early tillers and hunters
of sea-set Greece, looking at the Pleiades in winter,
Alcyone in its lovely group suggested the Nest
of the Halcyon, the summer-bird who had flown
to the remote depths of the sky to sit and brood
there on a windless wave-unreached nest till once
again "the Halcyon days" of calm settled on
land and sea: or to know that to our own sea-
faring folk of old, the men who voyaged perilously
in small and frail craft without compass and with

little knowledge of the mysterious laws of the
mysterious forces of earth and sea and heaven.
Polaris was the one unchanging skyey beacon,
the steadfast unswerving North Star; and so,
lovingly called by our old Saxon forbears the
*Scipsteorra*, the Ship-Star, and by the Elizabethan
seafarers the Lodestar or Pilot-Star, and by the
Hebridean fishermen the Home-Star, and by others
the Star of the Sea:

Constellations come, and climb the heavens, and go,
Star of the Pole! and thou dost see them set.
       Alone in thy cold skies,
Thou keep'st thy old unmoving station yet,
   Nor join'st the dances of that glittering train,
Nor dipp'st thy virgin orb in the blue western main.
      On thy unaltering blaze
The half-wrecked mariner, his compass lost,
     Fixes his steady gaze,
And steers, undoubting, to the friendly coast;
And they who stray in perilous wastes by night
Are glad when thou dost shine to guide their footsteps
   right.

The same spirit which animated Bryant when
he wrote these verses in his beautiful " Hymn to
the North Star," which made one of the Gaelic
island-poets allude to it as the Star of Compassion,
prevailed with these Chaldæan shepherds and
Arabian nomads of old. They gave the familiar
or beautiful names of love or intimate life, and
in exchange the taciturn face of heaven lost its
terrifying menace of silence, and the Night became
a comrade, became the voice of the poets, of the
sages, of the prophets and seers, the silver gateways
of the Unknown.

The Hunter, The Herdsman, the Bear-Watcher,
the Driver of the Wain—how much more we love
Boötes, or, as Chaucer called the constellation,
" ye sterres of Arctour," because of these simple
names. The Herdsman, the Hunter, . . . the
words strike the primitive music. The youth of
the world is in them. In these few letters what
infinite perspectives, what countless images. The
Golden Age lies hid in their now impenetrable
thickets. Through their branches we may look
at the tireless hunter of to-day on the interminable
pampas, at the bowed trailer in the dim savannahs
of the Amazon, at the swarthy nomad on the
wastes of Sahara guarding his camels like ships
becalmed in a vast sea of sand, or may see the
solitary mountain-shepherd in the hill-wildernesses
of Spain or Italy, or the Northern herdsman toiling
against wind and snow on our Gaelic hills.

Here also is the romance of the stars, as well
as that deeper and perturbing romance which
is disclosed to us in the revelations of science.
That sense of incalculable distances, of immeasure-
able periods, of unknown destinies and amazing
arrivals, which haunts the imagination of the
astronomer when he looks beyond the frontiers
of ascertained knowledge, half-doubting perhaps
whether even that be not an illusory logic, is also
here. One goes back, as in thought one recedes
into the beautiful, impassioned wonderland of
childhood. One seems to see mankind itself as a
child, gone but a little way even yet, looking up

trustfully or fearfully to the mysterious mother-eyes of a Face it cannot rightly discern, in its breath being Immortality, Eternity in its glance, and on its brows Infinitude.

II

Of all winter stars surely the most familiar is Polaris, the Pole Star or Lodestar: of all winter constellations, the Plough, the Little Dipper (to give the common designations), Orion, and the lovely cluster of the Pleiades, are, with the Milky Way, the most commonly observed stellar groups. One of our old Scottish poets, Gawain Douglas, writing towards the close of the fifteenth or early in the sixteenth century, thus quaintly brought them into conjunction:

> Arthurys hous, and Hyades betaikning rane,
> Watlingstrete, the Horne and the Charlewane,
> The fiers Orion with his goldin glave.

Here possibly he has taken Arcturus for Polaris. Of old, the Lodestar and Arcturus (or, as often given in the North, "Arturus" or "Arthur" . . . a word itself signifying the Great or Wondrous Bear) were often confused. Sometimes, too, Arcturus stood for the whole constellation of Ursa Major—or, as we commonly call it, the Plough or the Wain, as, for example, in Scott's lines:

> Arthur's slow wain his course doth roll,
> In utter darkness, round the Pole.

But it is obvious Gawain Douglas did not mean this to be understood, for in the second line he

169

speaks of "Charlewane," *i.e.*, Charles's Wain
. . . the Wain or Waggon being then, as it still
is among country-folk, even more familiar a term
than the Great Bear or than the Plough itself.
Probably, then, he had in mind the Pole Star,
the "House of Arthur" of the ancient British.
His choice of the "rain-betokening Hyades"
may be taken here as including the Pleiades,
these "greater seven" in whom centres so much
poetry and old legend. A previous paper has been
devoted to the Milky Way, so that there is no
need to explain why Watling Street should be
analogous with the Galaxy. The "Horne" is
the Little Dipper or Ursa Minor. Than "fierce
Orion with his glistering sword" there is no
constellation so universally familiar. If, then, to
this category of the old Scottish poet, we add the
star Aldebaran, and the constellation of Taurus
or the Bull, we have more than enough Winter
Lights to consider in one chapter.

Having already, however, dealt with "the
watery constellations" we can be the more content
now to ignore Alcyone, Maia, Taygeta, Electra,
and the other Pleiadic stars of Taurus. This great
constellation is one of the earliest in extant
astronomical records: the earliest, it is believed.
The stellar image of a Bull has occurred to many
nations since the designations first arose among
the ancient Cretans or Akkadians—if, indeed,
in its origin it was not immeasurably more remote.
East and West, in the deserts of the South and

among the grey isles of the North, " the Bull "
was recognised. To-day the Scottish peasant still
calls it " the Steer," as his German kinsman does
in *der Stier*, his French kinsman in *le Taureau*,
his Spanish or Italian kinsman in *Toro*. When
certain of the Greeks and Latins used *Keráon*
and *Cornus* instead of *Tauros* and *Taurus*, they
said merely the same thing—the Horned One.
Virgil, as many will remember, utilises the image
in the first *Georgic*:

> When with his golden horns bright Taurus opes
> The year . . .

just as a poet of our own time, in a beautiful
" Hymn to Taurus," writes:

> . . . I mark, stern Taurus, through the twilight grey
> The glinting of thy horn
> And sullen front, uprising large and dim
> Bent to the starry Hunter's sword at bay.

Among our own ancestors, the Druids made
Taurus an object of worship, the Tauric Festival
having been one of the great events of the year,
signalised when the sun first entered the imagined
frontiers of this constellation. To-day, among the
homesteads of our Scottish lowlands, the farm-
folk tell of the Candlemas Bull who may be seen
to rise in the gloaming on New Year's Eve and
move slowly to the dark pastures which await
his coming.

The particular stellar glory of this constellation
is Aldebaran. This beautiful star has appealed
to the imagination of all peoples. I do not know

what were its earliest Celtic or Anglo-Saxon names. But as in Gaelic it is sometimes called "the Hound," this term may well be a survival from ancient days. If so there is an interesting relation with the primitive Arabic name by which it is all but universally known. Aldebaran is *Al Dabarān*, the Follower: and, figuratively, a follower could hardly be better symbolised than by a hound. I recall a Gaelic poem on a legendary basis where the analogy is still further emphasised, for there Aldebaran is called "the Hound of the Pleiades," which is exactly what the Arabian astronomers implied in "the Follower." Another interesting resemblance is between "the red hound" of the Gaelic poet and legend and the *Rohinī* of the Hindus, the word signifying "a red deer" . . . in each case the ruddy gleam of the star having suggested the name. Probably it was this characteristic which led Ptolemy to apply to the star the name "Lampadias" or the Torch-Bearer. In the narration of folk-tales I have more than once or twice heard Aldebaran alluded to as the star of good fortune, of "the golden luck." With us it is pre-eminently a winter-star, and may be seen at its finest from the latter part of January till the approach of the vernal equinox. Some idea of its luminosity may be gained from the fact that this is thrice the outglow of the Pole Star. How often I have stood on a winter's night, and watched awhile this small red "torch" burning steadfastly in the unchanging heavens, and thought of its vast journeys, of that eternal, appalling procession through the infinite deeps: how often I have felt the thrill of inexplicable mystery when, watching its silent fire in what appears an inexorable fixity, I recall what science tells us, that it is receding from our system at an all but unparalleled velocity, a backward flight into the unknown at the rate of thirty miles a second.

It would be hopeless to attempt here even the briefest account of the primitive and diverse nomenclature, the mythology, the folklore of Orion . . . the Winter-Bringer, as this constellation is called in an old Scandinavian saga, identical thus with the marginal reading in the Geneva Bible relative to the reference to Orion in Job—" which starre bringeth in winter," an allusion to its evening appearance at the season of cold and storms. For these things are writ in the records of a hundred nations. They are alive in the poetry of all peoples. Centuries before our era, when Thebes was the greatest city of Greece, the poetess Corinna sang of this great Warrior, the Great Hunter, whose nightly course was so glorious above the dusky lands and waters of Hellas. Long after Pindar and the Greek poets, Catullus and Horace gave it a like pre-eminence in Latin literature. In our own poetry, many surely will recall from *Paradise Lost*:

> . . . when with fierce winds Orion arm'd
> Hath vext the Red-sea coast, whose waves o'erthrew
> Busiris and his Memphian chivalry . . .

or Tennyson's beautiful line in *Locksley Hall*:

Great Orion sloping slowly to the west . . .

or, it may be, that epic of *Orion* upon which is based Richard Hengist Horne's claim to re-membrance—or, once more, Matthew Arnold's fine allusion to Sirius and Orion in *Sohrab and Rustum* :

. . . the Northern Bear,
Who from her frozen height with jealous eye
Confronts the Dog and Hunter in the South.

Before Catullus or Pindar the Egyptians had identified Orion both with Horus and Osiris. Among the peoples of Israel the poets acclaimed the constellation as Nimrod, " the mighty Hunter " (or by another term signifying the Giant), " bound to the sky for rebellion against Jehovah." Among the Celtic races it has had kindred names, some-times abstract, sometimes personal, as the Gaelic Fionn. A year or so ago I was told a sea-tale of the Middle Isles, in which was an allusion to this constellation as " the Bed of Diarmid." This is of especial interest, because of its connection with Fionn or Finn, the Nimrod, the great Hunter of the Gael. But in this story (a modern, not an ancient tale, though with more than one strange old survival) the major position is not held by Fionn, but by the Alban-Gaelic hero Diarmid, who is represented as succumbing under the spear thrust in his left side by the enraged Fionn, at last in grips with the daring chieftain who had robbed him of Grania. When questioned, my informant said he had heard a variant of this attribution, and that the constellation was an image of Diarmid with Grania hanging to his side in a swoon, because she and her lover have been overtaken by the wrath of Fionn . . . though from the description I was uncertain whether the latter indicated the star Sirius, or the rival constellation of the Great Bear. The Gaels of old called Orion *Caomai*, a name said to signify the Armed King: while the Gall (the Scandinavian races) applied the name *Orwandil*, but with what signification I do not know, though I have read somewhere that it stood for Hero, or for an heroic personage.

Of the chief stars in Orion there is not space here to speak. But of the splendid Rigel—as affluent in the mysterious science of the astrologer as in nocturnal light—pearly Anilam, of the Belt or Sword—ominous Belatrix—ruddy-flamed Betelgeuze—of these alone one might write much . . . as one might write much of the Girdle or Staff itself, what Scott in *The Lay of the Last Minstrel* calls " Orion's studded belt." It has a score of popular names, from the Danish *Frigge Rok* (Freya's Distaff) to the seamen's " Yardarm," as, collectively, its three great stars have all manner of names in different countries, from the Magi, or the Three Kings or the Three Marys, to the Rake of the French Rhinelanders, or the Three Mowers of the Silesian peasant.

Those who have studied the mythology and folklore of the Pleiades will remember how universally the numeral seven is associated with their varying nomenclature. But there was, and still is among primitive peoples, not infrequent confusion in the use of "The Seven Stars" as a specific name. Although from China to Arabia, from India and Persia to the Latin countries of the South, the term almost invariably designates the Pleiades, in the folklore of many Western nations it is used for the seven planets, and in many Northern races it is often used for the seven brilliant stars of the Great Bear. Even the Biblical allusion to "The Seven Stars," as our own Anglo-Saxon ancestral *Sifunsterri*, does not necessarily indicate the Pleiades: many consider the seven great planets to be meant. There is a Shetland rune, common to all the north isles and to be heard in Iceland and Norway, known as the rune of sevens, and of which one of the invocatory lines is "And by da seven shiners." All kinds of interpretation have explained this, from the obvious "seven planets," or else the Pleiades, to the Seven Candlesticks of Revelation and I know not what besides. I have again and again asked fisher-folk or others from the Orkneys and Shetlands, and in all but one or two instances the answer has clearly indicated the Great Bear, occasionally Polaris and the Ursine Arcturus and their nearest brilliant "shiners." Again, *Crannarain*, one of the Gaelic names for the Pleiades,

is, perhaps, as often applied to the Great Bear:
the curious legend of the Baker's Shovel, implied
in the Gaelic term, fitting equally.

Of the Great Bear, of the North Star, however,
I have already spoken. Of Polaris itself, indeed,
there is more than enough to draw upon. It is
strange that "the Lamp of the North" should
have so fascinated all the poets from the time
of Homer till to-day, and yet that all have dwelled
in the same illusion as to its absolute steadfastness.
Nevertheless, Homer's

> Arctos, sole star that never bathes in the ocean wave

has both poetic truth and the truth of actuality.

It is a relief to put aside notes and pen and
paper, and to go out and look up into the darkness
and silence, to those "slow-moving palaces of
wandering light" of which one has been writing.
How overwhelmingly futile seems not only the
poor written word, but even the mysterious pursuit
of the far-fathoming thought of man. By the sweat
of the brow, by the dauntless pride of the mind,
we mortal creatures have learned some of the
mysteries of the coming and going in infinitude of
these incalculable worlds, of their vast procession
from the unknown to the unknown. Then, some
night, one stands solitary in the darkness, and
feels less than the shadow of a leaf that has passed
upon the wind, before these still, cold, inevitable,
infinitely remote yet overwhelmingly near Children
of Immortality.

# THE DEATH OF SWINBURNE

## By Ernest Rhys

RETURNING from France on the night of Swinburne's funeral, we bought the English papers upon landing, and there and then read in full the news that had reached us so far only in a schoolboy's letter. As we went on then to London, I and my fellow-traveller, who had known him well, tried in vain to realise that he had that day made his last journey through the English shires, to be buried at Bonchurch, and that the familiar house on Putney Hill would see him no more. "The greatest of our lyrical poets," George Meredith called him in a letter to their common friend there, which we found printed in one of the evening papers. With a like sense of his genius and unprecedented powers, we had yet never quite learnt to range him with his contemporaries, having rather thought of him as one of the classic poets of an earlier world than as the child and true creature of the nineteenth century. Rightly to celebrate his memory and estimate his loss, one ought to have something of his own princely excess in love and grief for his heroes, as when, at the death of Victor Hugo in the spring of 1885, he wrote of the incalculable debt he owed to the master who had fostered whatever nobler passions and aspirations he could command "with the bread of his deathless word and the wine of his immortal song." But to make prose sing is not given to the ordinary mortal, who must be content to call up in sober memory the place and effect of the poets he has known, and leave the rest to their own great accents.

When Victor Hugo died, all Paris joined in the funeral train that bore the remains to the Pantheon. When his English disciple died, how little was London moved! One cannot but reflect on the difference, seeing that Swinburne was a rarer lyric poet than Hugo (in spite of his own contrary belief), if Hugo's inferior in drama and in certain other forms of art that both attempted. The difference was not only one marking off the two peoples; it was as much one between the two poets. Hugo had sung liberty and the sea and the sea-wind, and wild nature, very much as his disciple had done; but he had been and he remained a poet of human nature and of the men and women of Paris up to the end; and the men and women had learnt to recognise his voice. Swinburne after the climacteric year, 1879, was no longer a poet of men and women at all, unless we consider little children, of whom he became the laureate, as men and women. He had become to all intents and purposes a poet of nature. Living near London, he forgot London; gave himself up to surprising nature day by day through all the changes of the year on its neighbouring heaths and commons, and to writing poems of memory or present ecstasy, or songs of those creatures who with him were content with green grass, a May tree, and a blue sky.

One of the most distinct memories I have of him goes back to a day in May, when I heard him describe to a guest the new-come lustre of a hawthorn tree, blossoming on Wimbledon Common. Not one of the poems he wrote dealing with the theme, and written about the same time, conveys quite the rapturous reality of his words in describing it to the blue-eyed listener at his side, who had possibly been incredulous about any wilder charms that could linger unspoilt so near London and its smoke. The long, solitary morning expeditions over two commons that gave him these delights were scarcely ever intermitted. Of later years these rambles were always solitary, and during them he saw nothing but the grass, the trees, the sky—and his fellow-rhapsodists, small children. Even if he met friends he did not recognise them: a lady, an old friend of his, one morning purposely stood right in his path, to see if he would stop and speak to her. But he simply bowed his head, without noticing who the interrupter was, and passed on.

The incident would not be worth telling if it was not so characteristic of him in his older years; living so near London, yet so aloof from it; absorbed in his own thoughts and the spectacle of nature; envisaging men more and more as a fief of nature, not nature as a religion and dominion of man.

His affection from boyhood for certain English places and wilder countrysides, Northumbrian moors and southern sea-coasts, was of a part with this creed. It was bound up, too, just as closely with his love of England herself, and with a hatred, furious, unreasoning, profane, of her enemies, upon whom he could not shower epithets enough of rage and anathema. For, like other men of genius, he was made up of opposites. With all his spirit of revolt, he was an aristocrat of a hundred inherited prejudices; while he was to the end a hot republican, he was just as fierce a conservative. How should a school, humorous, self-conscious, that dealt in comparatives and subtleties, understand an old poet whose hopes, fears, passions, memories, rages, were all cast in superlatives?

This is, I admit, to suggest a picture of an intellectual Berserker that does not quite tally with the familiar order of his days as they were lived under the roof of his inseparable friend and fellow-poet, Theodore Watts-Dunton, which kept an even tenor enough as time went on.

A five-mile ramble under the open sky, during which he thought out and completely shaped down to the last line any poem he had in his mind, so that afterwards it was written down without the change of a syllable; a return then to a late lunch party with two or three favourite guests, when he was as sociable, witty, as full of interest in the newspapers and events of the day as before he had been self-absorbed and solitary; and an evening of books and bookish delights, when often some newly discovered quarto, say a play of Dekker's or Webster's, was opened between the tall candlesticks by whose light he invariably read.

Old books, and best of all old play books, were never to him, what they seem to the multitude, soulless things, closed testaments of dead men. They were communicative and enlivening companions. It was so when he was a boy, as we know by the uncontrollable excitement he showed over a copy of Victor Hugo's *Notre-Dame*, which, carried home to Capheaton in his school holidays, gave him his first Hugo fever. It was so up to the very end, as one realised in watching him over his beloved quartos and the plays that he wrote about in his sonnets on the Elizabethan dramatists, including unconsidered trifles like *Doctor Dodypol* and *Nobody and Somebody*.

Who in our time has known those forgotten dramatists as did he—Haughton, Barnes, blithe, burly Porter, rough Rowley, light Nabbes, lean Sharpham, "soft Davenport, sad-robed, and Brome, gipsy-led across the woodland ferns"? The room that housed these treasures, his own special sanctum, was walled and enveloped in books, those of his own earlier contemporaries included. There were Robert Browning's poems, and Dante Rossetti's, and Sir Henry Taylor's

*Philip van Artevelde*. The influence of Browning and Rossetti faded out of his pages as he advanced; but that of the latter, and of the mediæval French poets he loved, was shown in Swinburne's tribute to his translation from Villon, *The Ballad of the Ladies of Old Time*, " so incomparably rendered," so far beyond any feat of the younger poets in that way. It was to be seen in the influence of pictures like *Bocca Baciata* upon his own painted rhymes and mediæval fantasies.

The influence of Rossetti in his poems as well as his pictures, his theory of art, exorbitant and all-engrossing, his neo-Romanticism and his Italianate temper, upon Swinburne cannot very well be over-estimated. It gave stimulus to his early imagination; did him a master's inestimable service, did him possibly, too, some human damage.

Having admitted this, we have to remember that *Atalanta in Calydon*, still among his longer poems his masterpiece, was mainly written under Rossetti's roof, and that it shows remarkably little trace of him. There is more of his influence in *Chastelard* ; much more in some of the poems and ballads. Swinburne spoke of *Chastelard* in later days with amused contempt as a play conceived and partly written by a younger poet only half escaped from the college walls; but it recalls Rossetti's studio too.

Swinburne left Oxford in 1858 or 9, having already there made acquaintance with William Morris and other congenial spirits. His first book,

*The Queen-Mother and Rosamund*, published in 1861, is crude and often imitative, but it is magically informed with the spirit of poetry; and there are lines in *Rosamund* that show how he was reading his Elizabethans, and seeking for a mode suited to his own imaginative conceit and sense of words.

> I that have held a land between twin lips
> And turned large England to a little kiss;
> God thinks not of me as contemptible.

But it is clear, as one looks back, that the writer of these ardent plays, although he confessed that his first ambition and his most urgent was to do something not unworthy of " a young countryman of Marlowe the teacher and Webster the pupil of Shakespeare," was much more strongly moved by lyrical than by dramatic impulses. He conceives his scenes as pictures or as songs; his people are wonderfully set in the stage scene. But it is rare that they speak individually, or from innate dramatic compulsion. They are like people figured in tapestry, and it is the poet behind the arras, and swaying them as he moves to and fro, whose emotional, monotonously heightened voice we hear.

This image occurs to one naturally as a result of having heard the poet at any time read or recite any poem of his aloud. The unusual volume and sonority of his voice heard in an ordinary room like his study at the " Pines " were startling on a first experience. I remember hearing him read *Ex Voto*,

and at first feeling almost overwhelmed by the
orchestral tones, as he chanted, verse by verse:

> When their last hour shall rise
> Pale on these mortal eyes
> Herself like one that dies,
>    And kiss me dying
> The cold last kiss, and fold
> Close round my limbs her cold
> Soft shade as raiment rolled,
>    And leave them lying,
>
> If aught my soul would say
> Might move to hear me pray
> The birth god of my day
>    That he might hearken,
> This grace my heart should crave,
> To find no landward grave
> That worldly springs make brave,
>    World's winters darken.

First printed in *The Athenæum*, *Ex Voto* is one
of the second series of " Poems and Ballads."
This must have been very near the dividing
equator in his career, the year when he began his
second stage; if we try to range now the stars of
his first period with those of the second, we have
to remember that, born in 1837, he published
in 1861 his first boyish book of plays ; went on
with his dramatic studies in *Chastelard*, in which
he was still feeling his way; then dropping it as
the lyric impulse supervened, wrote *Atalanta in
Calydon*, one of the few really supremely great
things done in poetry in all the century, and one
which proved triumphantly that he had found his
way. So far his masters are clearly enough to
be distinguished. Shakespeare, Browning and

ERNEST RHYS

Rossetti are the chief influences in the first three plays; Æschylus, Landor and Shelley all certainly helped him to speed his mingled lyric and dramatic imagination in *Atalanta*.

Meanwhile he was writing some of the " Poems and Ballads " that were to shake the coteries and provoke a storm of criticism. In this book, the guiding spirits are much mingled; black, white and grey ; classic, mediæval and modern; they included Sappho, Catullus, Lucretius, Gautier, Baudelaire, Hugo, and again Rossetti, and again Browning. One cannot wonder that the book was attacked, though the mode and incidency of the attack were unworthy, seeing that it came from a fellow-poet who had put on a mask and a Mother Shipton's cap for the occasion.

In this book we see that he was not merely a writer gifted with extraordinary music and imagination, but he was, like some other lyric poets, led by emotions, not by ideas; and his ideas were too often caught up only when his flying machine was about to start. The same impulsiveness marked him as a political rebel. There he owed his first lesson in individual liberty to a very early master, his grandfather, Sir John Swinburne of Capheaton, who had been a friend of Mirabeau and who lived to be near a hundred without abating a jot of his Viking courage and contempt for expedient ways of thought. One hears the old man eloquent once and again in the poems; it is his voice that sounds, speaking to the impetuous boy, standing wide-eyed at his knee, in *Songs before Sunrise*:

> *Master, what of the night?*
>    Child, night is not at all
>    Anywhere, fallen or to fall,
> Save in our star-stricken eyes,
> Forth of our eyes it takes flight,
>    Look we but once nor before
> Nor behind us, but straight on the skies,
>    Night is not there any more.

We have to take the one break for liberty with the other. The same indifference to customary sentiment that marked his first book of the ecstasy and liberty of love gave him his charter in going to Italy and becoming fired by the ardour of the liberators there. His *Song of Italy*, inscribed " with devotion and reverence " to Mazzini, is the first book of this testament of his to the European struggle for the life and soul of a race.

As inspiriting a pæan of a hero ever sung, the *Song of Italy* yet shows one of the besetting snares of its writer, caused by excess of the lyrical over the logical impulse. The poem is a third longer than its ideal argument demands. Four years later came, however, *Songs before Sunrise*, the one book in which the ideas and the emotions act and react musically and intrinsically upon one another; in which the " War of Liberation of Humanity," to use Arnold's phrase, seemed to find once and for all its English voice. The very dialect of liberty seems to be enlarged by this noble book, which breathes a humane and a religious ardour, a love of and a longing for morning light and a hatred of darkness, not to be found elsewhere unless it be in his especial masters, Shelley at home or Hugo abroad. And at the end of the music, how does the soldier and trumpeter of the new day remember that he is a lover too?

> Ask nothing more of me, sweet;
>   All I can give you I give,
> Heart of my heart, were it more——
> More would be laid at your feet:
>   Love that should help you to live,
> Song that should spur you to soar.

On the shelf *Bothwell* succeeds *Songs before Sunrise*, and in this magnificently impossible drama, his *drame épique*, as he termed it in the dedication to Victor Hugo—the poem which, like Spenser's *Faerie Queene*, no one reads right through; the play which no theatre will ever play—Swinburne took his revenge on the public, much as Browning did with *Sordello*. Nevertheless, a play written with a strong hand, in which the minds of men are better expressed than they are themselves, considered as dramatic forces. They all speak, for one thing, in a lofty monotone; the hands may be the hands of Bothwell or Darnley; the voice is always Swinburne's. Mary Queen of Scots is most euphuist when she is most moved; a mistake in art.

>             Why should love
> Have not the force to pluck but twelve hours back
> And twice consume and twice consummate life,
> Twice crowned and twice confounded?

But the blank verse is often magnificent, and one of the best dreams ever wrought into the woof of tragedy is Darnley's dream in the second act.

*Bothwell* was half written in London, in the poet's rooms in Great James Street, and while he was living its life, as he had written his play, with a characteristically reckless expense of nervous energy. He studied closely the town, delighting in its streets, its playhouses, its queerest haunts from " Solferino's " to the " Coal Hole." We know how he went to the Marston nights, much favoured of young poets and critics, *Noctes Ambrosianæ* that began at twelve and went on till daylight broke in on the revellers. He became, because of his unconventional personal effect and his joyous indifference to public opinion, the scapegoat of the æsthetic movement, to whom every myth of Bohemia attached itself. Villon's companions and Marlowe's cronies were his, according to the lurid legend: he ate strange flesh, drank blood, spat fire, and read the works of Jeremy Taylor in bed at half-past three in the afternoon.

The wonder is that his highly-strung, over-susceptible frame, whose nerves seemed to have been fed on quicksilver, ever stood it. As a matter of fact, they did not stand it. Judging by what his shrewd physician, Dr. George Bird, who often saw him in those days, said of him, one gathers that he was in danger of hopeless neurasthenia when he left London in 1879.

ERNEST RHYS

All the while he was maintaining his art with an apparently undiminished flow of books. His novel, *A Year's Letters*, was running through *The Tatler* in 1876–77; his *Essays and Studies*, full of characteristically extravagant appreciation and daring heresy, appeared in 1875, and the same year saw his essay on *George Chapman*. In the former volume, his first real prose testament, he showed not only his love of those poets, his chosen masters, who were gone, but a generous zeal for the work of his contemporaries. In his tribute to Coleridge, and in other vehement essays, he uttered some of those sayings which became proverbial and passed into the Victorian currency. In its pages he arrived at his favourite division of the Titans and the Olympians: " Sometimes a supreme poet is both at once: such, above all men, is Æschylus: so also Dante, Michel Angelo, Shakespeare, Milton, Goethe, Hugo, are gods at once and giants; they have the lightning as well as the light of the world, and in hell they have commands as in heaven; they can see in the night as by day."

In 1875, when *Essays and Studies* appeared, he had already made the acquaintance of a fellow-critic who was destined considerably to affect his mind as time went on; and four years later he went to live with him at Putney.

This friend, Theodore Watts-Dunton, was an evolutionist among the æsthetes, who had a theory all his own, and could prove to Rossetti that his inspiration was not really pre-Raphaelite, and offer

Swinburne the post of lay clerk of nature in his new cosmogony. He acted as a conductor of the new ideas which Darwin, Herbert Spencer, Huxley and others were then busily expounding; and pointed the way from a mere eclectic æstheticism to a faith in which a passion for the sea and a sense of the joy of earth were not incidental, but demanded by ideal logic. This seems to have given Swinburne's imagination a new impetus: it resolved some of the erratic atoms in his make-up, and gave them a nucleus.

These new ideas, it may be said, have tended to destroy the romantic spirit. But Swinburne, born a poet and made a romanticist, could not forgo his birthright: and as it happened his new guide was a romanticist too who could show the two spirits not incompatible. Every great English poet has touched, or longed to treat at one time or another, Celtic romance. Swinburne had fallen under its charm in his turn, and the spell was that of the magic of Iseult, the Essylt of the Welsh tales, the Isolde of Wagner's lyric drama; but the poem she inspired is inspired by the goddess too.

Long before, reading Boccaccio, and searching for a vehicle in which to make Italian romance run delicately in English verse, the poet had tried and found good Dryden's narrative couplet. *The Two Dreams*, in the first series of "Poems and Ballads," is the prelusive strain to the later music of *Tristram of Lyonesse*. But the pace of the first is but tardy compared with the later poem.

# ERNEST RHYS

The lavish music and sumptuous verbal beauty of the love-passages in this romance of Cornwall and Brittany mark both the rapture and the self-indulgence of its writer's sensuous art. But the scene at the close where Tristram lies wounded, and in his despair confers with the other Iseult of Brittany, shows a rarer control of the instrument.

In *Tristram of Lyonesse* Swinburne had consciously gathered up all his powers for a decisive achievement. He had seen the mastersingers, his contemporaries, one after another take up Celtic romance, and deal finely and accordantly with it after their manner. But he was not quite satisfied with any of their modern settings. Certainly he did not find the idyllic grace of the *Idylls of the King* to his mind. But Matthew Arnold's delightful Tristram poem, which he rated much higher, had stirred in him a spirit of emulation, and Wagner's *Tristan und Isolde*, one of the few things in modern music that had appealed to him—for he had little ear for music apart from verse—served to decide the impulse. His unaffected delight at the accomplishment of the theme may be read in the sonnet of dedication he prefaced to it:

> Life stands crowned
> Here with the best one thing it ever found,
> As of my soul's best birthdays dawns the third.

Whether it was before writing *Tristram* or after that he went with Principal Jowett to Cornwall, and visited Tintagel and the sea scenes that figure

192

n the romance drawn from that wild coast, I am not sure. Poets have sometimes been content to figure first the scenes in art that they have gone to nature to confirm or not afterwards. If this were taken to imply that Swinburne did not study, and for that matter too paint, his chosen subjects in *plein air*, the suggestion would be libellous. He lived half his days out of doors, and what he did not know about some of the wilder coasts of England, north and south, would not be worth recovering. And one of the essential qualities of *Tristram* comes of the glorious conceit of the sea and the wilder elements as enlarging the wild passions of men.

*Tristram* was written yesterday, as it might seem, for a generation in literature is like a day. But a change in the spirit of poetry and in the current of thought has come about since then, and one is not sure how they affect the achievements of a generation ago. The importance of the romance in Swinburne's history cannot be overlooked because in it we see the amorist and love-romancer passing at recurring moments into the new style romanticist, the first articles of whose faith were written by Wordsworth and Shelley. After this, his genius was more and more deliberately given over to the nature-poetry and the religious rhapsodies of earth, sea and sky, which were, as he fondly hoped and believed, to complete his greater testament.

In his last books are many noble poems which

express his curious pantheism. Needless to tell, what so many of these later pages show, that his sea-obsession, too, lasted and never lost its force. Guy de Maupassant has narrated for us one of his early adventures at Etretat, which helped, it is said, to inspire *Ex Voto*, and in which Swinburne (who always secretly hoped to die at last by drowning) all but lost his life.[1]

What is to be said of the poet who lies buried by the seacoast he loved, at Bonchurch? What will time, the great decider of men's labour and fame, eventually say of him? We are too near him to judge with any certainty how he will appear to those who look back to him as he looked back to Coleridge and Shelley. But it is hard to believe that any change of the perspective will dim the brightness of his lyric achievement. He was

[1] " One morning some sailors gave the alarm, crying out that a swimmer was drowning under La Porte d'Amont. They took a boat, and I went with them. The swimmer, not knowing the terrible current that runs there, had been drawn in, but luckily picked up by a fishing boat behind the Petite Porte. I learnt the same evening that the imprudent bather was an English poet, M. Algernon Charles Swinburne, who had been staying for a few days with a M. Powell, owner of a little *châlet* that he had baptised Chaumière Dolmancé." This M. Powell had astonished the country by a life solitary and bizarre. The two foreigners asked M. de Maupassant to join them at *déjeuner* next day: and he found them in a pretty garden behind a low house built of flint and thatched. Both were of small stature, M. Powel fat, Swinburne thin, and surprising at a first glance,—indeed, in the guest's eyes a most fantastic apparition that reminded him of Edgar Poe.

prodigal of his music, that new music he had taught the old tongue; over-prodigal at times, seeing that verse may run once too often in the triple-lilt of his magical cadences. But he has left English poetry reinforced at point after point, where he used his strength on his real themes; he was religious in his worship of nature, and if pantheism ever built a church, he would help to furnish its litany.

# "MARY BARTON"

## By Thomas Seccombe

*Mary Barton* belongs to the romance of nineteenth-century fiction; prose fiction under Victoria took the place of Elizabethan drama, and legend has clustered round the first books of those who made the nineteenth-century novel illustrious in England. Like *Pickwick, Jane Eyre, Adam Bede, The Warden,* and *Richard Feverel, Mary Barton* was a first serious attempt; like them, too, it was never entirely surpassed by more mature work, and even in an age which produced *Alton Locke, Sybil, Les Misérables,* and the *Christmas Carol,* in the strength of its compassion and the power of the plea that it makes for the poor, *Mary Barton* remains unrivalled. It is more intimate in its knowledge, it is a more accurate mirror of the life which it reflects than any competitor, and what seems perhaps to make it more exceptional still is the fact that this portrayal of poverty emanated from a comely and happy-conditioned married woman of thirty-seven, whose experience of the woe, the weariness, and the transience of human life one would have surmised to have been anything but profound.

Born at Chelsea in September 1810, Elizabeth Stevenson lost her mother at thirteen months, and was taken to live with her mother's sister —Aunt Lumb—her "more than mother," who dwelt in a tall red house on Knutsford Heath. As a child she was happy there, even though her aunt—whose means were circumscribed—had to practise in her modest household some of those elegant economics immortalised in *Cranford*, and at school in Stratford-on-Avon. At the age of seventeen she returned home to Chelsea, where her unhappiness under the *régime* of her father's second wife is probably faintly reflected in *Wives and Daughters*. There in April 1829 her father— a versatile, rather erudite, conscientious, and, we should imagine, rather easily domineered-over man—died, leaving by his second wife a son and a daughter, Catherine (Cynthia). His death terminated a two years of bondage and affliction for the elder daughter, who in a few months returned to Knutsford. During the next three years she made long visits to Newcastle, where she was connected with a Unitarian minister of considerable eminence, the Rev. William Turner (the original of Thurstan in *Ruth*). She also stayed with the Ramseys at Edinburgh, and with some of her Holland cousins in Essex. Little more than three years elapse from her father's death, and in the August of 1832 we find the beautiful Miss Stevenson framed for life as the wife of the Rev. William Gaskell, junior minister of the Cross Street

Chapel in Manchester; he was twenty-seven and she was barely twenty-two. The chapel was situated in the storm centre of the desperate industrial conflict of the cruel thirties and hungry forties. To get a scientific picture of the life of, and the habitations occupied by, the poor in Manchester during the cruel thirties and hungry forties, one must read *The Condition of the Working Class in England in* 1844, by Frederick Engels, and Dr. J. P. Kay's *Moral and Physical Condition of the Working Classes employed in the Cotton Manufacture in Manchester*. The description of the cattle sheds for human beings in the working-class portion of the city, and of the abominations attendant upon the overcrowding, and the emanations from the sewer-like rivers of Manchester, are too disgusting to be quoted here. Here is one of the least repulsive passages, describing the cottages in a spot known as Little Ireland, immediately south of the Oxford Road, Manchester, in a curve of the Medlock, surrounded on all sides by tall factories, within about half a mile of the Cross Street Chapel. The description applies to the whole period in which the incidents of *Mary Barton* are cast:

The cottages are old, dirty, and of the smallest sort, the streets uneven, fallen into ruts, and in parts without drains or pavement; masses of refuse, offal, and sickening filth lie among standing pools in all directions; the atmosphere is poisoned by the effluvia from these, and laden and darkened by the smoke of a dozen tall factory chimneys. A horde of ragged women and children swarm about here, as filthy as the swine that thrive upon the garbage heaps and in the puddles. In short, the whole rookery furnishes such a hateful and repulsive spectacle as can hardly be equalled in the worst courts on the Irk. The race that lives in these ruinous cottages, behind broken windows, mended with oilskin, spring doors, and rotten door-posts, or in dark, wet cellars, in measureless filth and stench, in this atmosphere penned in as if with a purpose, this race must really have reached the lowest stage of humanity. This is the impression and the line of thought which the exterior of this district forces upon the beholder. But what must one think when he hears that in each of these pens, containing at most two rooms, a garret, and perhaps a cellar, on the average twenty human beings live; that in the whole region, for each one hundred and twenty persons, one usually inaccessible privy is provided; and that in spite of all the preachings of the physicians, in spite of the excitement into which the cholera epidemic plunged the sanitary police by reason of the condition of Little Ireland, in spite of everything, in this year of grace 1844, it is in almost the same state as in 1831! Dr. Kay asserts that not only the cellars but the first floors of all the houses in this district are damp; that a number of cellars once filled up with earth have now been emptied once more by Irish people; and are occupied once more by Irish people; that in one cellar the water constantly wells up through a hole stopped with clay, the cellar lying below the river level, so that its occupant, a hand-loom weaver, had to bale out the water from his dwelling every morning and pour it into the street!

Twelve years after her happy marriage Mrs. Gaskell became a mother for the fourth time, and a few months later lost her only son, named William after father and grandfather. Coming on the top of the distress and starvation incidental to the strikes and lock-outs—of which she had been a witness—the blow for a time unsteadied her. Her husband had noticed that literary composition acted upon her as a sort of anodyne; he had discovered this in the course of several small experiments both in prose and verse which they had undertaken together. He now prescribed a work of larger scope and ambition, and placed at his wife's disposal much of his own laboriously garnered experience. The result was the production of *Mary Barton*, the composition of which occupied twelve months of absorbed but not uninterrupted work, and with intervals it occupied the whole of 1846 and 1847. Exactly midway between *Sybil* and *Alton Locke*, *Mary Barton* was published in two volumes under the pseudonym of " Cotton Mather Mills " in the early autumn of 1848. The publishers kept it for some months before they realised that the book had a strong topical interest, and then offered the author to purchase the copyright for £100, which was gladly accepted. The year, of course, was the year of revolution, the *annus mirabilis*, which witnessed among other things the fall to earth of July monarchy, the success of *Vanity Fair*, and the utter failure of the People's Charter— the Manchester school had killed it. *Mary Barton* was a pathetic plea for the vanquished: theoretically it amounted to little more than a variation on Samuel Bamford's pitiful lament " God help the poor "; but it irritated the rich millowners and the professors of the dismal science, who could find no place for the poor in their philosophy save under the euphemisms of labour and supply. In the history of ideas, *Mary Barton* will always occupy a noble place as the starting-point and rallying-cry of a new generation of Humanitarians, following that wave which had in England expended its energy upon slave emancipation.

But it is more than that. It is a starting-point in the history of the novel, and as a work of art I cannot think that Mrs. Gaskell, with all her experience, ever surpassed it. It was written under a strong pressure of emotion. It is impregnated by profound human sympathy, tender and true. An unpretentious appeal by a new writer to the hearts of the multitude, it struck home equally as a revelation and as a plea for the down-trodden. And it achieved this result largely by a subordination both of purpose and of personality to a virtually new conception of the novel as a harmonious work of art. Manchester was observed, one might almost say perceived for the first time, by a "foreigner" who was yet thoroughly acclimatised and knew her subject. The characters, originally drawn from life, were carefully subdued to the requirements of the story. The plot had slowly engraved itself upon the same plate with the *dramatis personæ* in the writer's mind. Light and shadow are skilfully arranged, thought and emotion alternate, nothing is exaggerated, no side is taken, no sermon preached, no personality obtruded. Mrs. Gaskell was content to sink herself and to remain absorbed, her idiosyncrasy temporarily suspended in her work. She wrote a limpid style unhampered by any affectation or bizarrerie. Her dialogue is natural and spontaneous, her local colour fresh and unstudied. Her sympathies are deep, womanly, thoughtful, thoroughly normal. The result is a limitation, an economy, and a balance. The world is startled and surprised at being so taken by a simple thing. But it is no small thing, then or now, to have written a fragrant, healthy, ethical, English novel, which appealed to a world as wide as that addressed by either Scott or Dickens. " Forcible," " fair," and even " terrible " in its truth, are epithets employed by *The Athenæum* in its review of 21st October, 1848.

The achievement admitted Mrs. Gaskell at once to the front rank of Victorian novelists. The three fairy gifts of fiction, knowledge of human nature, a good story, and a good style, were hers from the outset. The gods dowered her with right plots for her novels, and her descriptive powers were such that she could conjure up a tea-party given by one Lancashire operative to another with all the light and shade and glow of simple life and health and appetite of a real Dutch master. She touches the heart with instant force in the story of Old Alice.[1]

---

[1] She had told the story in part before, in verse, in *Blackwood* for January 1837. In *Libbie Marsh*, too, she had already shown what she could do in pathetic idyll.

I was young and thoughtless, and thought it was a fine thing to go so far from home. So, one day, th' butcher he brings us a letter fra George, to say he'd heard on a place—and I was all agog to go, and father was pleased like; but mother said little, and that little was very quiet. I've often thought she was a bit hurt to see me so ready to go—God forgive me! But she packed up my clothes, and some o' the better end of her own as would fit me, in yon little paper box up there—it's good for nought now, but I would liefer live without fire than break it up to be burnt; and yet it's going on for eighty years old, for she had it when she was a girl, and brought all her clothes in it to father's, when they were married. But, as I was saying, she did not cry, though the tears was often in her eyes; and I seen her looking after me down the lane as long as I were in sight, with her hand shading her eyes—and that were the last look I ever had on her.

The book is certainly a marvel of receptivity. It not only champions the poor; it describes them at pretty close quarters. It begins with a nice topographical touch describing Green Heys Fields, the site to-day of Moss Side Library, and Green Hay House, historical as the residence of De Quincey and J. A. Froude. The Ancoats tea-party, the fire at the mill, the picture of "Old Alice" (countrywoman of "Poor Susan," proto-type of "Old Sally" in *Ruth* and "Old Betty" in *Phillis*), the succouring of the Davenports, the connoisseurship of Job Legh, the sailor's return, the pursuit of the *John Cropper*—all these are scenes observed at first hand, verified and supplemented by the observation and know-ledge of her husband. The conception of John

Barton with his Burns-like hatred and contempt of the rich—

Like a do-nothing lady, worrying shopmen all morning, and screeching at her pianny all afternoon, and going to bed without having done a good turn to any one of God's creatures.

Thou never could abide the gentlefolk.

And what good have they ever done me! If I am sick, do they come and nurse me? If my child lies dying . . .

A country fellow at the pleugh,
His acres till'd, he's right eneugh . . .
But Gentlemen, an' Ladies warst,
Wi' ev'ndown want o' wark are curst. .
They loiter, lounging, lank and lazy;
Tho' deil haet ails 'em, yet uneasy:
Their days insipid, dull an' tasteless,
Their nights unquiet, lang an' restless.

—may have been suggested, I think, by a working-man counter-type of such characters in Scott as Balfour of Burley and Major Bridgenorth in *Peveril*. The conception was quickened and confirmed by the gesture of a typical operative of that day who put his hand on her arm when she was visiting and asked if *she* had ever had a child clemm'd to death. The central features of the murder (fixed up by lot) and the trial at Liverpool Assizes were suggested by the Ashton case of 1834. In chapters thirty-three, thirty-four, and especially thirty-seven, there is a good deal of padding due to the publishers' nefarious pronunciamento that the book must be bulked out some six thousand words beyond its original length. Wayward and impulsive and, at times, nervously apprehensive as she was in her composition, Mrs. Gaskell clearly owed much in her work to a calm but decided domestic criticism. Her husband, it must be remembered, was one of those wise and well-doing, restful and serene, yet at the same time widely-instructed pastors which Unitarianism at its best produces and has produced in most abundance in the Palatine and West Riding.

*Mary Barton*, when all deductions are made, is one of the greatest novels of compassion that our country has produced. It ranks Mrs. Gaskell with Goldsmith, Hood, Dickens, and Mark Rutherford as one of the truest and most pathetic protectors of the poor. This story of shirtings can move us not less than the " Song of a Shirt "— the " Chanson de la Chemise " of which a French critic writes succinctly, " Elle obtint un grand succès, mais ne produisit aucun résultat." The praise of Miss Edgeworth, Miss Martineau, the Howitts, Bamford, Landor, Carlyle, Forster, and Dickens made the happy and beaming authoress quite a literary personage. Dickens clamoured for copy from her, and *Our Society at Cranford* was the result. This with *Cousin Phillis* and *Wives and Daughters* reveals the lighter, more idyllic and, at the same time, fun-reflecting side of her nature. She was always fond of the sketch structure. *Ruth* and *North and South* complete the working of the particular " pocket " of material which *Mary Barton* opened. *Sylvia's Lovers* stands apart, the sea-story of her early ambition, her greatest creative effort, perhaps her noblest work. But *Mary Barton* is first, in colouring, dramatic effect, and vividness, as the result of transcript from real life, unsurpassed by anything that she wrote during the whole of her eighteen years of production. She wrote it from a full heart. Most of our classical authoresses have been spinsters, childless. Mrs. Gaskell, a solitary exception, was the mother of a family and a pastor's wife as well. Where they speculated and imagined she observed and drew from the deep well of experience. When she describes the deaths of children, she feels what she has not merely seen, but, unlike our excellent Hannahs, Marias, Janes, Harriets, Charlottes, and Mary Annes, actually felt. She was at the time of an age evocative of deep feeling. Charged with the pathos of life and the ubiquity of premature death and suffering, the book is full of unforced tears. To me it seems likely to outlast anything she wrote. Already it has lasted well. Over sixty-three years have elapsed since it appeared. Forty-seven have passed since the great novelist died. At that time Mrs. Gaskell was just completing *Wives and Daughters*, for the serial rights of which she obtained £2000 (in lieu of the £100 given outright for *Mary Barton*). Desiring a more secluded kind of literary leisure than either Plymouth Grove or Silverdale afforded, she was arranging a secondary home for herself in the south, at Holybourne, a short two miles north-

east of Alton. The purchase was effected and Mrs.
Gaskell was discussing some detail, *in situ*, with
her daughters Meta, Florence, and Julia, and also
the husband of Florence, Charles Compton, Q.C.
It was a Sunday afternoon, 12th November, 1865.
Some of the party had gone to church, and it had
been remarked how well Mrs. Gaskell was looking.
Those at home were preparing tea in the drawing-
room to the accompaniment of a blazing early-
winter fire. Mrs. Gaskell was quoting to her
son-in-law something that his father—dead just
a fortnight before—had said, and it is a pathetic
coincidence that, if she had finished the sentence
in the process of utterance, her next words would
have been " when I am dead." Before she was able
to utter them she leaned forward and fell—dead.
Incomplete as *Wives and Daughters* was, it is the
most finished of all her works, and shows her
powers at their ripest. She was buried in the
graveyard of the little chapel in Brook Street,
Knutsford, which had been familiar from childhood,
and is faithfully described in *Ruth*. There, in June
1884, her husband was laid by her side.

# "DOMBEY AND SON"

## By G. K. Chesterton

In Dickens's literary life *Dombey and Son* represents a break so important as to necessitate our casting back to a summary and a generalisation. In order fully to understand what this break is, we must say something of the previous character of Dickens's novels, and even something of the general character of novels in themselves. How essential this is we shall see shortly.

It must be remembered that the novel is the most typical of modern forms. It is most typical of modern forms especially in this, that it is essentially formless. All the ancient modes or structures of literature were definite and severe. Any one composing them had to abide by their rules; they were what their name implied. Thus a tragedy might be a bad tragedy, but it was always a tragedy. Thus an epic might be a bad epic, but it was always an epic. Now in the sense in which there is such a thing as an epic, in that sense there is no such thing as a novel. We call any long fictitious narrative in prose a novel, just as we call any short piece of prose without any narrative an essay. Both these forms are really quite formless, and both of them are really quite modern. The difference between a good epic by Mr. John Milton and a bad epic by Mr. John Smith was simply the difference between the same thing done well and the same thing done badly. But it was not (for instance) like the difference between *Clarissa Harlowe* and *The Time Machine*. If we class Richardson's book with Mr. Wells's book it is really only for convenience; if we say that they are both novels we shall certainly be puzzled in that case to say what on earth a novel is. But the note of our age, both for good and evil, is a high poetical and largely illogical faith in liberty. Liberty is not a negation or a piece of nonsense, as the cheap reactionaries say; it is a belief in variety and growth. But it is a purely poetic and even a merely romantic belief. The nineteenth century was an age of romance as certainly as the Middle Ages was an age of reason. They liked to have everything defined and defensible; the modern world prefers to run some risks for the sake of spontaneity and diversity. Consequently the modern world is full of a phenomenon peculiar to itself—I mean the spectacle of small or originally small things swollen to enormous size and power. The modern world is like a world in which toadstools should be as big as trees, and insects should walk about in the sun as large as elephants. Thus, for instance, the shopkeeper, almost an unimportant figure in carefully ordered states, has in our time become the millionaire, and has

more power than ten kings. Thus again a practical
knowledge of nature, of the habits of animals
or the properties of fire and water, was in the old
ordered state either an almost servile labour or
a sort of joke; it was left to old women and game-
keepers and boys who went birds'-nesting. In
our time this commonplace daily knowledge has
swollen into the enormous miracle of physical
size, weighing the stars and talking under the sea.
In short, our age is a sort of splendid jungle in
which some of the most towering weeds and
blossoms have come from the smallest seed.

And this is, generally speaking, the explanation of the novel. The novel is not so much the
filling up of an artistic plan, however new or
fantastic. It is a thing that has grown from
some germ of suggestion, and has often turned out
much larger than the author intended. And this,
lastly, is the final result of these facts, that the
critic can generally trace in a novel what was the
original artistic type or shape of thought from
which the whole matter started, and he will
generally find that this is different in every case.
In one novel he will find that the first impulse
is a character. In another novel he will find that
the first impulse is a landscape, the atmosphere
of some special countryside. In another novel he
will find that the first impulse is the last chapter.
Or it may be a thrust with sword or dagger, it
may be a theology, it may be a song. Somewhere
embedded in every ordinary book are the five

or six words for which really all the rest will be written. Some of our enterprising editors who set their readers to hunt for banknotes and missing ladies might start a competition for finding those words in every novel. But whether or no this is possible, there is no doubt that the principle in question is of great importance in the case of Dickens, and especially in the case of *Dombey and Son*.

In all the Dickens novels can be seen, so to speak, the original thing that they were before they were novels. The same may be observed, for the matter of that, in the great novels of most of the great modern novelists. For example, Sir Walter Scott wrote poetical romances before he wrote prose romances. Hence it follows that, with all their much greater merit, his novels may still be described as poetical romances in prose. While adding a new and powerful element of popular humours and observation, Scott still retains a certain purely poetical right—a right to make his heroes and outlaws and great kings speak at the great moments with a rhetoric so rhythmical that it partakes of the nature of song, the same quite metrical rhetoric which is used in the metrical speeches of Marmion or Roderick Dhu. In the same way, although *Don Quixote* is a modern novel in its irony and subtlety, we can see that it comes from the old long romances of chivalry. In the same way, although *Clarissa* is a modern novel in its intimacy and actuality, we can see that it comes from the old polite letter-writing and polite essays of the period of *The Spectator*. Any one can see that Scott formed in *The Lay of the Last Minstrel*, the style that he applied again and again afterwards, like the reappearances of a star taking leave of the stage. All his other romances were positively last appearances of the positively last Minstrel. Any one can see that Thackeray formed in fragmentary satires like *The Book of Snobs* or *The Yellowplush Papers* the style, the rather fragmentary style, in which he was to write *Vanity Fair*. In most modern cases, in short (until very lately, at any rate), the novel is an enormous outgrowth from something that was not a novel. And in Dickens this is very important. All his novels are outgrowths of the original notion of taking notes, splendid and inspired notes, of what happens in the street. Those in the modern world who cannot reconcile themselves to his method— those who feel that there is about his books something intolerably clumsy or superficial — have either no natural taste for strong literature at all, or else have fallen into their error by too persistently regarding Dickens as a modern novelist and expecting all his books to be modern novels. Dickens did not know at what exact point he really turned into a novelist. Nor do we. Dickens did not know, in his deepest soul, whether he ever really did turn into a novelist. Nor do we. The novel being a modern product is one of the few things to which we really can apply that disgusting

method of thought—the method of evolution.
But even in evolution there are great gaps, there
are great breaks, there are great crises. I have
said that the first of these breaks in Dickens may
be placed at the point when he wrote *Nicholas
Nickleby*. This was his first serious decision to
be a novelist in any sense at all, to be anything
except a maker of momentary farces. The second
break, and that a far more important break, is
in *Dombey and Son*. This marks his final resolution
to be a novelist and nothing else, to be a serious
constructor of fiction in the serious sense. Before
*Dombey and Son* even his pathos had been really
frivolous. After *Dombey and Son* even his absurdity
was intentional and grave.

In case this transition is not understood, one
or two tests may be taken at random. The episodes
in *Dombey and Son*, the episodes in *David Copperfield*, which came after it, are no longer episodes
merely stuck into the middle of the story without
any connection with it, like most of the episodes
in *Nicholas Nickleby*, or most of the episodes
even in *Martin Chuzzlewit*. Take, for instance,
by way of a mere coincidence, the fact that three
schools for boys are described successively in
*Nicholas Nickleby*, in *Dombey and Son*, and in
*David Copperfield*. But the difference is enormous.
Dotheboys Hall does not exist to tell us anything about Nicholas Nickleby. Rather Nicholas
Nickleby exists entirely in order to tell us about
Dotheboys Hall. It does not in any way affect

his history or psychology; he enters Mr. Squeers's school and leaves Mr. Squeers's school with the same character, or rather absence of character. It is a mere episode, existing for itself. But when little Paul Dombey goes to an old-fashioned but kindly school, it is in a very different sense and for a very different reason from that for which Nicholas Nickleby goes to an old-fashioned and cruel school. The sending of little Paul to Dr. Blimber's is a real part of the history of little Paul, such as it is. Dickens deliberately invents all that elderly pedantry in order to show up Paul's childishness. Dickens deliberately invents all that rather heavy kindness in order to show up Paul's predestination and tragedy. Dotheboys Hall is not meant to show up anything except Dotheboys Hall. But although Dickens doubtless enjoyed Dr. Blimber quite as much as Mr. Squeers, it remains true that Dr. Blimber is really a very good foil to Paul; whereas Squeers is not a foil to Nicholas; Nicholas is merely a lame excuse for Squeers. The change can be seen continued in the school, or rather the two schools, to which David Copperfield goes. The whole idea of David Copperfield's life is that he had the dregs of life before the wine of it. He knew the worst of the world before he knew the best of it. His childhood at Dr. Strong's is a second childhood. Now for this purpose the two schools are perfectly well adapted. Mr. Creakle's school is not only, like Mr. Squeers's school, a bad school, it is a bad

influence upon David Copperfield. Dr. Strong's
school is not only a good school, it is a good
influence upon David Copperfield. I have taken
this case of the schools as a case casual but con-
crete. The same, however, can be seen in any of
the groups or incidents of the novels on both
sides of the boundary. Mr. Crummles's theatrical
company is only a society that Nicholas happens
to fall into. America is only a place to which
Martin Chuzzlewit happens to go. These things
are isolated sketches, and nothing else. Even
Todgers's boarding-house is only a place where
Mr. Pecksniff can be delightfully hypocritical.
It is not a place which throws any new light on
Mr. Pecksniff's hypocrisy. But the case is different
with that more subtle hypocrite in *Dombey and
Son*—I mean Major Bagstock. Dickens does
mean it as a deliberate light on Mr. Dombey's
character that he basks with a fatuous calm in
the blazing sun of Major Bagstock's tropical and
offensive flattery. Here, then, is the essence of
the change. He not only wishes to write a novel;
this he did as early as *Nicholas Nickleby*. He
wishes to have as little as possible in the novel
that does not really assist it as a novel. Previously
he had asked with the assistance of what incidents
could his hero wander further and further from
the pathway. Now he has really begun to ask
with the assistance of what incidents his hero
can get nearer and nearer to the goal.

The change made Dickens a greater novelist.

I am not sure that it made him a greater man.
One good character by Dickens requires all eternity
to stretch its legs in; and the characters in his
later books are always being tripped up by some
tiresome nonsense about the story. For instance,
in *Dombey and Son*, Mrs. Skewton is really very
funny. But nobody with a love of the real smell
of Dickens would compare her for a moment,
for instance, with Mrs. Nickleby. And the reason
of Mrs. Skewton's inferiority is simply this, that
she has something to do in the plot; she has to
entrap or assist to entrap Mr. Dombey into
marrying Edith. Mrs. Nickleby, on the other
hand, has nothing at all to do in the story, except
to get in everybody's way. The consequence is
that we complain not of her for getting in everyone's way, but of everyone for getting in hers.
What are suns and stars, what are times and
seasons, what is the mere universe, that it should
presume to interrupt Mrs. Nickleby? Mrs. Skewton (though supposed, of course, to be a much
viler sort of woman) has something of the same
quality of splendid and startling irrelevancy. In
her also there is the same feeling of wild threads
hung from world to world like the webs of gigantic
spiders; of things connected that seem to have
no connection save by this one adventurous
filament of frail and daring folly. Nothing could
be better than Mrs. Skewton when she finds herself, after convulsions of speech, somehow on the
subject of Henry VIII., and pauses to mention

with approval " his dear little peepy eyes and his benevolent chin." Nothing could be better than her attempt at Mahomedan resignation when she feels almost inclined to say " that there is no What's-his-name but Thingummy, and What-you-may-call-it is his prophet!" But she has not so much time as Mrs. Nickleby to say these good things, also she had not sufficient human virtue to say them constantly. She is always intent upon her worldly plans, among other things upon the worldly plan of assisting Charles Dickens to get a story finished. She is always " advancing her shrivelled ear " to listen to what Dombey is saying to Edith. Worldliness is the most solemn thing in the world; it is far more solemn than other-worldliness. Mrs. Nickleby can afford to ramble as a child does in a field, or as a child does to laugh at nothing, for she is like a child innocent. It is only the good who can afford to be frivolous.

Broadly speaking, what is said here of Mrs. Skewton applies to the great part of *Dombey and Son*, even to the comic part of it. It shows an advance in art and unity; it does not show an advance in genius and creation. In some cases, in fact, I cannot help feeling that it shows a falling off. It may be a personal idiosyncrasy, but there is only one comic character really prominent in Dickens, upon whom Dickens has really lavished the wealth of his invention, and who does not amuse me at all, and that character is Captain Cuttle. But three great exceptions must be made

to any such disparagement of *Dombey and Son*.
They are all three of that divine order in Dickens's
creation which can no more be described or
criticised than strong wine. The first is Major
Bagstock, the second is Cousin Feenix, the third
is Toots. In Bagstock Dickens has blasted for
ever that type which pretends to be sincere by
the simple operation of being explosively obvious.
He tells about a quarter of the truth, and then
poses as truthful because a quarter of the truth
is much simpler than the whole of it. He is the
kind of man who goes about with posers for Bishops
or for Socialists, with plain questions to which he
wants a plain answer. His questions are plain
only in the same sense that he himself is plain—
in the sense of being uncommonly ugly. He is
the man who always bursts with satisfaction
because he can call a spade a spade, as if there
were any kind of logical or philosophical use in
merely saying the same word twice over. He is
the man who wants things down in black and white,
as if black and white were the only two colours;
as if blue and green and red and gold were not
facts of the universe. He is too selfish to tell the
truth and too impatient even to hear it. He cannot
endure the truth, because it is subtle. This man
is almost always like Bagstock—a sycophant and a
toad-eater. A man is not any the less a toad-eater
because he eats his toads with a violent appetite
and gobbles them up, as Bagstock did his breakfast, with the eyes starting out of his purple face.

He flatters brutally. He cringes with a swagger. And men of the world like Dombey are always taken in by him, because men of the world are probably the simplest of all the children of Adam.

Cousin Feenix again is an exquisite suggestion, with his rickety chivalry and rambling compliments. It was about the period of *Dombey and Son* that Dickens began to be taken up by good society. (One can only use vulgar terms for an essentially vulgar process.) And his sketches of the man of good family in the books of this period show that he had had glimpses of what that singular world is like. The aristocrats in his earliest books are simply dragons and griffins for his heroes to fight with—monsters like Sir Mulberry Hawk or Lord Verisopht. They are merely created upon the old principle, that your scoundrel must be polite and powerful—a very sound principle. The villain must be not only a villain, but a tyrant. The giant must be larger than Jack. But in the books of the Dombey period we have many shrewd glimpses of the queer realities of English aristocracy. Of these Cousin Feenix is one of the best. Cousin Feenix is a much better sketch of the essentially decent and chivalrous aristocrat than Sir Leicester Dedlock. Both of the men are, if you will, fools, as both are honourable gentlemen. But if one may attempt a classification among fools, Sir Leicester Dedlock is a stupid fool, while Cousin Feenix is a silly fool —which is much better. The difference is that the silly fool has a folly which is always on the border-land of wit, and even of wisdom; his wandering wits come often upon undiscovered truths. The stupid fool is as consistent and as homogeneous as wood; he is as invincible as the ancestral darkness. Cousin Feenix is a good sketch of the sort of well-bred old ass who is so fundamentally genuine that he is always saying very true things by accident. His whole tone also, though exag-gerated like everything in Dickens, is very true to the bewildered good nature which marks English aristocratic life. The statement that Dickens could not describe a gentleman is, like most popular animadversions against Dickens, so very thin and one-sided a truth as to be for serious purposes a falsehood. When people say that Dickens could not describe a gentleman, what they mean is this, and so far what they mean is true. They mean that Dickens could not describe a gentleman as gentlemen feel a gentle-man. They mean that he could not take that atmosphere easily, accept it as the normal atmos-phere, or describe that world from the inside. This is true. In Dickens's time there was such a thing as the English people, and Dickens belonged to it. Because there is no such thing as an English people now, almost all literary men drift towards what is called Society; almost all literary men either are gentlemen or pretend to be. Hence, as I say, when we talk of describing a gentleman, we always mean describing a gentleman from

the point of view of one who either belongs to or
is interested in perpetuating that type. Dickens
did not describe gentlemen in the way that gentlemen describe gentlemen. He described them in
the way in which he described waiters, or railway
guards, or men drawing with chalk on the pavement. He described them, in short (and this we
may freely concede), from the outside, as he
described any other oddity or special trade.
But when it comes to saying that he did not
describe them well, then that is quite another
matter, and that I should emphatically deny.
The things that are really odd about the English
upper class he saw with startling promptitude
and penetration, and if the English upper class
does not see these odd things in itself, it is not
because they are not there, but because we are all
blind to our own oddities; it is for the same reason
that tramps do not feel dirty, or that niggers do
not feel black. I have often heard a dear old
English oligarch say that Dickens could not
describe a gentleman, while every note of his
own voice and turn of his own hand recalled Sir
Leicester Dedlock. I have often been told by
some old buck that Dickens could not describe a
gentleman, and been told so in the shaky voice
and with all the vague allusiveness of Cousin
Feenix. Cousin Feenix has really many of the
main points of the class that governs England.
Take, for an instance, his hazy notion that he is
in a world where everybody knows everybody;

whenever he mentions a man, it is a man " with
whom my friend Dombey is no doubt acquainted."
That pierces to the very helpless soul of aristocracy.

Take again the stupendous gravity with which
he leads up to a joke. That is the very soul of the
House of Commons and the Cabinet, of the high-
class English politics, where a joke is always
enjoyed solemnly. Take his insistence upon the
technique of Parliament, his regrets for the time
when the rules of debate were perhaps better
observed than they are now. Take that wonderful
mixture in him (which is the real human virtue
of our aristocracy) of a fair amount of personal
modesty with an innocent assumption of rank.
Of a man who saw all these genteel foibles so
clearly it is absurd merely to say without further
explanation that he could not describe a gentleman. Let us confine ourselves to saying that he
could not describe a gentleman as gentlemen like
to be described.

Lastly, there is the admirable study of Toots,
who may be considered as being in some ways
the masterpiece of Dickens. Nowhere else did
Dickens express with such astonishing insight and
truth his main contention, which is that to be
good and idiotic is not a poor fate, but, on the
contrary, an experience of primeval innocence,
which wonders at all things. Dickens did not
know, any more than any great man ever knows,
what was the particular thing that he had to
preach. He did not know it; he only preached it.

But the particular thing that he had to preach was this: That humility is the only possible basis of enjoyment. That if one has no other way of being humble except being poor, then it is better to be poor and to enjoy. That if one has no other way of being humble except being imbecile, then it is better to be imbecile, and to enjoy. That is the deep, unconscious truth in the character of Toots—that all his externals are flashy and false; all his internals unconscious, obscure and true. He wears loud clothes, and he is silent inside them. His shirts and waistcoats are covered with bright spots of pink and purple, while his soul is always covered with the sacred shame. He always gets all the outside things of life wrong, and all the inside things right. He always admires the right Christian people, and gives them the wrong Christian names. Dimly connecting Captain Cuttle with the shop of Mr. Solomon Gills, he always addresses the astonished mariner as " Captain Gills." He turns Mr. Walter Gay, by a most improving transformation, into " Lieutenant Walters." But he always knows which people upon his own principles to admire. He forgets who they are, but he remembers what they are. With the clear eyes of humility he perceives the whole world as it is. He respects the Game Chicken for being strong, as the Game Chicken ought to be respected for being strong. He respects Florence for being good, as even Florence ought to be respected for being good.

And he has no doubt about which he admires most; he prefers goodness to strength, as do all masculine men. It is through the eyes of such characters as Toots that Dickens really sees the whole of his tales. Toots is perhaps the only man, except Dickens, who enjoys everything that happened in the story of *Dombey and Son*.

# A DEFENCE OF NONSENSE

## By G. K. Chesterton

THERE are two equal and eternal ways of looking at this twilight world of ours: we may see it as the twilight of evening or the twilight of morning; we may think of anything, down to a fallen acorn, as a descendant or as an ancestor. There are times when we are almost crushed, not so much with the load of the evil as with the load of the goodness of humanity, when we feel that we are nothing but the inheritors of a humiliating splendour. But there are other times when everything seems primitive, when the ancient stars are only sparks blown from a boy's bonfire, when the whole earth seems so young and experimental that even the white hair of the aged, in the fine biblical phrase, is like almond trees that blossom, like the white hawthorn grown in May. That it is good for a man to realise that he is " the heir of all the ages " is pretty commonly admitted; it is a less popular but equally important point that it is good for him sometimes to realise that he is not only an ancestor, but an ancestor of primal antiquity; it is good for him to wonder whether he is not a hero, and to experience ennobling doubts as to whether he is not a solar myth.

The matters which most thoroughly evoke this sense of the abiding childhood of the world are those which are really fresh, abrupt, and inventive in any age; and if we were asked what was the best proof of this adventurous youth in the nineteenth century, we should say, with all respect to its portentous sciences and philosophies, that it was to be found in the rhymes of Mr. Edward Lear and in the literature of nonsense. *The Dong with the Luminous Nose*, at least, is original, as the first ship and the first plough were original.

It is true in a certain sense that some of the greatest writers the world has seen—Aristophanes, Rabelais, and Sterne—have written nonsense; but unless we are mistaken, it is in a widely different sense. The nonsense of these men was satiric—that is to say, symbolic; it was a kind of exuberant capering round a discovered truth. There is all the difference in the world between the instinct of satire, which, seeing in the Kaiser's moustaches something typical of him, draws them continually larger and larger; and the instinct of nonsense which, for no reason whatever, imagines what those moustaches would look like on the present Archbishop of Canterbury if he grew them in a fit of absence of mind. We incline to think that no age except our own could have understood that the Quangle-Wangle meant absolutely nothing, and the Lands of the Jumblies were absolutely nowhere. We fancy that if the account of the knave's trial in *Alice in Wonderland* had been published in the seventeenth century it would have been bracketed with Bunyan's *Trial of Faithful* as a parody on the state prosecutions of the time. We fancy that if *The Dong with the Luminous Nose* had appeared in the same period every one would have called it a dull satire on Oliver Cromwell.

It is altogether advisedly that we quote chiefly from Mr. Lear's *Nonsense Rhymes*. To our mind he is both chronologically and essentially the father of nonsense; we think him superior to Lewis Carroll. In one sense, indeed, Lewis Carroll has a great advantage. We know what Lewis Carroll was in daily life: he was a singularly serious and conventional don, universally respected, but very much of a pedant and something of a Philistine. Thus his strange double life in earth and in dreamland emphasises the idea that lies at the back of nonsense—the idea of *escape*, of escape into a world where things are not fixed horribly in an eternal appropriateness, where apples grow on pear trees, and any odd man you meet may have three legs. Lewis Carroll, living one life in which he would have thundered morally against any one who walked on the wrong plot of grass, and another life in which he would cheerfully call the sun green and the moon blue, was, by his very divided nature, his one foot on both

worlds, a perfect type of the position of modern
nonsense. His Wonderland is a country populated
by insane mathematicians. We feel the whole
is an escape into a world of masquerade; we feel
that if we could pierce their disguises, we might
discover that Humpty Dumpty and the March
Hare were Professors and Doctors of Divinity
enjoying a mental holiday. This sense of escape
is certainly less emphatic in Edward Lear, because
of the completeness of his citizenship in the world
of unreason. We do not know his prosaic biography
as we know Lewis Carroll's. We accept him as
a purely fabulous figure, on his own description
of himself:

> His body is perfectly spherical,
> He weareth a runcible hat.

While Lewis Carroll's Wonderland is purely
intellectual, Lear introduces quite another element
—the element of the poetical and even emotional.
Carroll works by the pure reason, but this is not
so strong a contrast; for, after all, mankind in
the main has always regarded reason as a bit of a
joke. Lear introduces his unmeaning words and
his amorphous creatures not with the pomp of
reason, but with the romantic prelude of rich hues
and haunting rhythms.

> Far and few, far and few,
> Are the lands where the Jumblies live

is an entirely different type of poetry to that
exhibited in *Jabberwocky*. Carroll, with a sense

of mathematical neatness, makes his whole poem a mosaic of new and mysterious words. But Edward Lear, with more subtle and placid effrontery, is always introducing scraps of his own elvish dialect into the middle of simple and rational statements, until we are almost stunned into admitting that we know what they mean. There is a genial ring of common sense about such lines as:

> For his aunt Jobiska said " Every one knows
> That a Pobble is better without his toes,"

which is beyond the reach of Carroll. The poet seems so easy on the matter that we are almost driven to pretend that we see his meaning, that we know the peculiar difficulties of a Pobble, that we are as old travellers in the " Gromboolian Plain " as he is.

Our claim that nonsense is a new literature (we might almost say a new sense) would be quite indefensible if nonsense were nothing more than a mere æsthetic fancy. Nothing sublimely artistic has ever arisen out of mere art, any more than anything essentially reasonable has ever arisen out of the pure reason. There must always be a rich moral soil for any great æsthetic growth. The principle of *art for art's sake* is a very good principle if it means that there is a vital distinction between the earth and the tree that has its roots in the earth; but it is a very bad principle if it means that the tree could grow just as well with its roots in the air. Every great literature has

always been allegorical—allegorical of some view
of the whole universe. The *Iliad* is only great
because all life is a battle, the *Odyssey* because
all life is a journey, the Book of Job because all
life is a riddle. There is one attitude in which we
think that all existence is summed up in the word
" ghosts "; another, and somewhat better one,
in which we think it is summed up in the words
*A Midsummer Night's Dream*. Even the vulgarest
melodrama or detective story can be good if it
expresses something of the delight in sinister
possibilities—the healthy lust for darkness and
terror which may come on us any night in walking down a dark lane. If, therefore, nonsense is
really to be the literature of the future, it must
have its own version of the Cosmos to offer; the
world must not only be the tragic, romantic, and
religious, it must be nonsensical also. And here
we fancy that nonsense will, in a very unexpected
way, come to the aid of the spiritual view of things.
Religion has for centuries been trying to make
men exult in the " wonders " of creation, but it
has forgotten that a thing cannot be completely
wonderful so long as it remains sensible. So long
as we regard a tree as an obvious thing, naturally
and reasonably created for a giraffe to eat, we
cannot properly wonder at it. It is when we
consider it as a prodigious wave of the living soil
sprawling up to the skies for no reason in particular
that we take off our hats, to the astonishment of
the park-keeper. Everything has in fact another

side to it, like the moon, the patroness of nonsense. Viewed from that other side, a bird is a
blossom broken loose from its chain of stalk, a
man a quadruped begging on its hind legs, a house
a gigantesque hat to cover a man from the sun,
a chair an apparatus of four wooden legs for a
cripple with only two.

This is the side of things which tends most truly
to spiritual wonder. It is significant that in the
greatest religious poem existent, the Book of Job,
the argument which convinces the infidel is not
(as has been represented by the merely rational
religionism of the eighteenth century) a picture
of the ordered beneficence of the Creation; but,
on the contrary, a picture of the huge and unde-
cipherable unreason of it. "Hast Thou sent the
rain upon the desert where no man is?" This
simple sense of wonder at the shapes of things,
and at their exuberant independence of our intellectual standards and our trivial definitions, is
the basis of spirituality as it is the basis of nonsense. Nonsense and faith (strange as the conjunction may seem) are the two supreme symbolic
assertions of the truth that to draw out the soul
of things with a syllogism is as impossible as to
draw out Leviathan with a hook. The well-
meaning person who, by merely studying the
logical side of things, has decided that "faith
is nonsense," does not know how truly he
speaks; later it may come back to him in the
form that nonsense is faith.

# THE INN

## By Edward Thomas

The night was dark and solid rain tumultuously
invested the inn. As I stood in a dim passage I
could see through the bar into the cloudy parlour,
square and white, surrounded by settles, each
curving about a round table made of one piece of
elm on three legs. A reproduction of " Rent Day "
and a coloured picture of a bold Spanish beauty
hung on the wall, which, for the rest, was suffi-
ciently adorned by the sharp shadows of men's
figures and furniture that mingled grotesquely.
All the men but one leaned back upon the settles
or forward upon the tables, their hands on their
tankards, watching the one who sang a ballad—
a ballad known to them so well that they seemed
not to listen, but simply to let the melody surge
about them and provoke what thoughts it would.

At some time, perhaps many times in his life,
every man is likely to meet with a thing in art or
nature or human life or books which astonishes and
gives him a profound satisfaction, not so much because it is rich or beautiful or strange, as because it
is a symbol of a thing which, without the symbol, he

could never grasp and enjoy. The German archers making a target of Leonardo's sculptured horse and horseman at Milan; the glory of purple that has flown from a painted church window and settled upon a peasant's shoulders for an hour; the eloquence, as of an epigram rich in anger and woe, of one bare branch that juts out from a proud green wood into the little midnight stars and makes them smaller with its splendid pang; a woodman felling one by one the black and golden oak trees in the spring and slaying their ancient shadows; or, in a discreet and massive crowd, one jet of laughter, so full of joy or defiance or carelessness that it seems to cut through the heavy air like the whistle of a bullet—the world is one flame of these blossoms, could we but see. Music has many of them in her gift. Music, the rebel, the martyr, the victor—music, the romantic cry of matter striving to become spirit—is itself such a symbol, and there is no melody so poor that it will not at some time or another, to our watchful or receptive minds, have its festal hour in which it is crowned or at least crucified, for our solemn delight. "Dolly Gray" I have heard sung all day by poor sluttish women as they gathered peas in the broad, burning fields of July, until it seemed that its terrible, acquiescent melancholy must have found a way to the stars and troubled them.

And of all music, the old ballads and folk songs and their airs are richest in the plain, immortal symbols. The best of them seem to be written in a language that should be universal, if only simplicity were truly simple to mankind. Their alphabet is small; their combinations are as the sunlight or the storm, and their words also are symbols. Seldom have they any direct relation to life as the realist believes it to be. They are poor in such detail as reveals a past age or a country not our own. They are in themselves epitomes of whole generations, of a whole countryside. They are the quintessence of many lives and passions made into a sweet cup for posterity. A myriad hearts and voices have in age after age poured themselves into the few notes and words. Doubtless, the old singers were not content, but we, who know them not, can well see in their old songs a kind of immortality for them in wanderings on the viewless air. The men and women—who hundreds of years ago were eating and drinking and setting their hearts on things—still retain a thin hold on life through the joy of us who hear and sing their songs, or tread their curving footpaths, or note their chisel marks on cathedral stones, or rest upon the undulating churchyard grass. The words, in league with a fair melody, lend themselves to infinite interpretations, according to the listener's heart. What great literature by known authors enables us to interpret thus by virtue of its subtlety, ballads and their music force us to do by their simplicity. The melody and the story or the song move us suddenly and launch us into an unknown. They are not art, they come to us imploring a new lease of life on the sweet earth, and so we come to give them something which the dull eye sees not in the words and notes themselves, out of our own hearts, as we do when we find a black hearthstone among the nettles, or hear the clangour of the joyous wild swan, invisible overhead, in the winter dawn.

In the parlour of the inn the singer stood up and sang of how a girl was walking alone in the meadows of spring when she saw a ship going out to sea and heard her true love crying on board; and he sailed to the wars and much he saw in strange countries, but never came back; and still she walks in the meadows and looks out to sea, though she is old, in the spring. He sang without stirring, without expression, except in so far as light and darkness from his own life emerged enmeshed among the deep notes. He might have been delivering an oracle of solemn but ambiguous things. And so in fact he was. By its simplicity and remoteness from life the song set going the potent logic of fancy which would lead many men to diverse conclusions. It excluded nothing of humanity except what baseness its melody might make impossible. The strangeness and looseness of its framework allowed each man to see himself therein, or some incident or dream in his life, or something possible to a self which he desired to be or imagined himself to be, or perhaps believed himself once to have been. There were no bounds of time or place. It included the love of Ruy

Blas, of Marlowe, of Dante, of Catullus, of Kilhwch, of Swift, of Palomides, of Hazlitt, of Villon. . . . And that little inn, in the midst of mountains and immense night, seemed a temple of all souls, where a few faithful ones still burnt candles and remembered the dead.

# THE CASTLE OF CARBONEK

## By Edward Thomas

THE castle stands high among vast, sharp-edged
waves of sand at the edge of a cliff, and looks at
the sea and a long, empty shore. At its feet a
little river can be seen running in a narrow valley.
A few miles off it rises in the red moorland, then
it falls with many a cascade down ladders of crag,
broadens among willows where long leaves are all
horizontal in the wind, and here by the castle
it has reached an elvish, merry old age already,
as it moves clear over the brown stones and out
among the rocks to the sea. Opposite the castle,
across the river, the other side of the valley is
clothed in dense and luminous oak wood. Where
the river joins the sea both the castle hill and the
wooded hill break away into a broken multitude
of bristling rocks, and among their alleys and
hidden corridors and halls the waves leap with
the motion of a herd of ridgy cattle galloping
through narrow gateways. Beyond, and away
for ten miles, the high dark coast sweeps in a
curve which the sea whitens by showing its teeth;
and round the headland at the end the ships come
and go at starry intervals. Landward, the country

rises in long, steep, furzy curves, interrupted by sudden rocks, to the red moor and the autumn evening sky of towering, tumultuous and yet steady grey cloud.

The castle stands among pale sand and long plumy grasses. The sand is deep within the hollow and roofless circuit of the broken walls, through which, here and there, come glimpses of sea or sky disconnected from any fragment of the land, that I seem to stand between the sea and sky. In the summer ivy-leaved toad-flax buds and harebells, most delicate flowers, whisper from the crevices. But nothing lives here now. The trunk of an old tree that once grew through the walls is now so much worn that what it was when it lived is not to be known. Not only is all human life gone from here, but even the signs of its decay are invisible. The noble masonry can suffer no more except at the hands of men; it is too low and too strong. It is a rude crag. Neither history nor legend speaks intelligently of it. It is but known that it was raised by hands, and each man that comes to it has to build it again out of his own life and blood, or it remains not far removed from nothing. The wayfarer starts at the sight of it, tries in vain, shuddering at the cliff and the desolate sea, to conceive a life lived by beings like himself in such a place. To have lived there men must have had fairy aids or the blood of witches or of gods in their veins.

Here might easily have been builded in a night

that phantom palace and its illusive pomps, where the Corinthian Lycius dwelt with the phantasmal Lamia until a philosopher's eye unbuilt it again.

Or on these sands might have stood Myratana and blind Tiriel before the beautiful palace, and cursed their sons.

Or up in the vanished high bowman's window the king's daughter sat and harped and sang:

> There sits a bird i' my father's garden,
>   An' O! but she sings sweet!
> I hope to live an' see the day
>   When wi' my love I'll meet.

When the sun has set, and land and sea are dissolved in cold mist, all but a circle of pale sand and the castle fragment, it seems true that here, to the foot of the tower that is gone, came the king's daughter and wept and sighed and made a great moan: "Ah! he mourns not who does not mourn for love." And the good king came and asked her if she desired to wed, and she answered, "Alas, sire, yes. Ah! he mourns not who does not mourn for love."

> Las! il n'a nul mal qui n'a le mal d'amour:
> Las! il n'a nul mal qui n'a le mal d'amour.
>   La fille du roi est au pied de la tour,
>   Qui pleure et soupire et mène grand dolour.
> Las! il n'a nul mal qui n'a le mal d'amour:
> Las! il n'a nul mal qui n'a le mal d'amour.
>   Le bon roi lui dit: Ma fille, qu'avez vous?
>   Voulez-vous un mari? Hélas! oui, mon seignoux.
> Las! il n'a nul mal qui n'a le mal d'amour:
> Las! il n'a nul mal qui n'a le mal d'amour.

Here, away from earth and sea and sky, apart

from men and time and any care, the melody and the picture are truer than before, suiting that melancholy wood, in which the heart, seeming to go back easily through unguessed deeps of time, makes all sorrows its own, airily, not without delight.

And there are others who abode here or abide here, as for example those timeless knights of no age or clime — Pelleas, Launcelot, Pellinore, Palomides, Galahad, whose armour no man pretends to show us, whom old men's tongues and poets' pens have lured into immortality—to whom this castle gives a home.

When Launcelot had come to the water of Morteise, says Malory, he slept, and there in a vision he was bidden to rise and put on his armour and enter the first ship that he found. And he did so, and the ship moved without sail or oar, and in the ship was great sweetness so that "he was fulfilled with all things that he thought on or desired." There he slept, and when he awoke there was none on board except the dead sister of Sir Percivale; and the ship went on for more than a month and Sir Launcelot fed on manna, until at last he touched land and there met Sir Galahad, his son. For half a year the two sailed together, and "often they arrived in isles far from folk, where there repaired none but wild beasts." But one day at the edge of a forest a white knight warned Sir Galahad that he should stay with his father no more. "And therewith Galahad entered into the forest. And the wind arose, and drove Launcelot more than a month throughout the sea, where he slept but little, but prayed to God that he might see some tidings of the Sangreal. So it befell on a night, at midnight, he arrived afore a castle, on the back side, which was rich and fair, and there was a postern opened toward the sea, and was open without any keeping, save two lions kept the entry; and the moon shone clear. Anon Sir Launcelot heard a voice that said: Launcelot, go out of this ship and enter into the castle, where thou shalt see a great part of thy desire. Then he ran to his arms, and so armed him, and so went to the gate and saw the lions. Then he set hand to his sword and drew it. Then there came a dwarf suddenly, and smote him on the arm so sore that the sword fell out of his hand. Then heard he a voice say: O man of evil faith and poor belief, wherefore trowest thou more on thy harness than in thy Maker, for He might more avail thee than thine armour, in whose service thou art set. Then said Launcelot: Fair Father Jesu Christ, I thank Thee of Thy great mercy that Thou reprovest me of my misdeed; now see I well that ye hold me for your servant. Then he took again his sword and put it up in his sheath, and made a cross in his forehead, and came to the lions, and they made semblaunt to do him harm. Notwithstanding he passed by them without hurt, and entered into the castle to the chief fortress, and there were they all at rest. Then Launcelot entered in so armed, for he found no gate nor door but it was open. And at the last he found a chamber whereof the door was shut, and he set his hand thereto to have opened it, but he might not.

" Then he enforced him mickle to undo the door. Then he listened and heard a voice which sung so sweetly that it seemed none earthly thing; and him thought the voice said: Joy and honour be to the Father of Heaven. Then Launcelot kneeled down before the chamber, for well wist he that there was the Sangreal within that chamber. Then said he: Fair sweet Father, Jesu Christ, if ever I did thing that pleased Thee, Lord, for Thy pity ne have me not in despite for my foule sins done afore-time, and that Thou show me something of that I seek. And with that he saw the chamber door open, and there came out a great clearness, that the house was as bright as all the torches of the world had been there. So came he to the chamber door and would have entered. And anon a voice said to him: Flee, Launcelot, and enter not, for thou oughtest not to do it; and if thou enter thou shalt forthink it. Then he withdrew him aback right heavy. Then looked he up in the middle of the chamber, and saw a table of silver, and the Holy Vessel, covered with red samite and many angels about it, whereof one held a candle of wax burning, and the other held a cross and the orna-ments of an altar. Ard before the Holy Vessel he saw a good man clothed as a priest. And it seemed that he was at the sacring of the mass.

And it seemed to Launcelot that above the priest's hands were three men, whereof the two put the youngest by likeness between the priest's hands; and so he lift it up right high, and it seemed to show so to the people. And then Launcelot marvelled not a little, for him thought the priest was so greatly charged of the figure that him seemed that he should fall to the earth. And when he saw none about him that would help him, then came he to the door a great pace, and said: Fair Father Jesu Christ, ne take it for no sin though I help the good man which hath great need of help. Right so entered he into the chamber, and came toward the table of silver; and when he came nigh he felt a breath, that him thought it was intermeddled with fire, which smote him so sore in the visage that him thought it brent his visage; and therewith he fell to the earth and had no power to arise; so he was so araged, that had lost the power of his body, and his hearing, and his seeing. Then felt he many hands about him, which took him up and bare him out of the chamber door, without any amending of his swoon, and left him there, seeming dead to all people. So upon the morrow when it was fair day they within were arisen, and found Launcelot lying afore the chamber door. All they marvelled how that he came in, and so they looked upon him, and felt his pulse to wit whether there were any life in him; and so they found life in him, but he might not stand nor stir no member that he had. And so they took him by every part of the body, and bare him into a chamber, and laid him in a rich bed, far from all folk; and so he lay four days. Then the one said he was alive, and the other said, nay. In the name of God, said an old man, for I do you verily to wit he is not dead, but he is so full of life as the mightiest of you all; and therefore I counsel you that he be well kept till God send him life again.

"In such manner they kept Launcelot four-and-twenty days and all so many nights, that ever he lay still as a dead man; and at the twenty-fifth day befell him after midday that he opened his eyes, and when he saw folk he made great sorrow, and said: Why have ye awaked me, for I was more at ease than I am now. O Jesu Christ, who might be so blessed that might see openly thy great marvels of secretness there where no sinner may be! What have ye seen? said they about him. I have seen, said he, so great marvels that no tongue may tell, and more than any heart can think, and had not my son been here afore me I had seen much more. Then they told him how he had lain there four-and-twenty days and nights. Then him thought it was a punishment for the four-and-twenty years that he had been a sinner, wherefore our Lord put him in penance four-and-twenty days and nights. Then looked Sir Launcelot afore him, and saw the hair which he had borne nigh a year, for that he forthought him right much that he had broken his promise unto the hermit, which he had avowed to do. Then they asked how it stood with him. Forsooth, said he, I am whole of body, thanked be Our Lord; therefore, sirs, for God's love tell me where I am. Then said they all that he was in the Castle of Carbonek."

And when the moon is clear, and the tingling sea is vast and alone, this castle on the sand above the grim coast is Carbonek, meet for all adventures and all dreams.

PRINTED BY
THE TEMPLE PRESS AT LETCHWORTH
IN GREAT BRITAIN